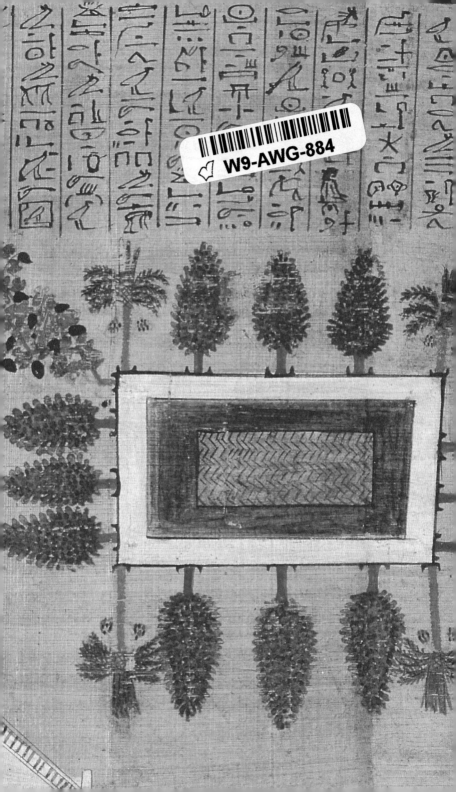

For Antonia

the
EGYPTIANS

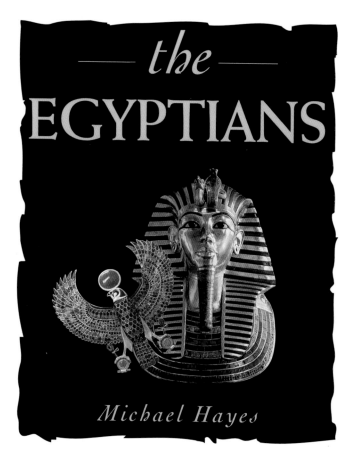

Michael Hayes

RIZZOLI
NEW YORK

Contents

Introduction

1. Gift of the Nile, Image of Heaven 8

Egypt and its seasons were shaped by the annual Nile flood.
The Egyptians responded to this by creating a complex magic
mythology centred on their gods and king.

2. The New Kingdom Begins — Lords of a Brave New World 28

A family of warrior kings and queens expelled foreign rulers
and took their armies beyond Egypt's borders.

3. By the Sunlit, Starlit Nile 48

Secure from any foreign threat, the Egyptians
settled down to ordinary life.

4. Temples, Festivals, Priests and Visions 74

Temples were built as homes for Egypt's gods. Priests cared for the gods
and their sacred images, organised great festivals in their honour and
shaped sacred spaces to channel the light of the universe.

Introduction

Heaven and earth conspired to bless the land of Egypt with constant sunny days and an annual flood which carpeted the Nile's banks with rich fertile soil. Each year, the Egyptians received a heavenly sign heralding the flood: the appearance, at dawn, of the night sky's brightest star, Sirius. Their religious and political imaginations, distant and safe from any foreign threat, responded to this miracle. They created a civilisation whose art and architecture still hold us enthralled today: the Pyramid Age — the Old Kingdom (*c.*2660–2125 BC).

However, after centuries, the energy, resources and will which had built the pyramids began to diminish. Egypt was distracted by civil strife. Order and stability were successfully returned to Egypt during the Middle Kingdom (*c.*2040–1782 BC). Egypt's rulers built pyramids again, but a new force was slowly entering Egypt, eventually to transform it. Foreign peoples from the Middle East were infiltrating Egypt's north-eastern frontier. They finally established themselves as the Hyksos kings of Egypt, "rulers from foreign places". They challenged Egypt's native rulers to the south, forming an alliance with African tribes further to the south.

The Egyptians felt themselves surrounded by enemies. They were humiliated. Their own rulers were killed in battle. Then they rose up against their foes and set out to save their country. Aided by their great queens, a dynasty of warrior pharaohs emerged to disentangle this alien hold on their beloved land. By *c.*1570 BC the heroic age of the New Kingdom had begun.

Equipped and armed with the new technologies and weapons they had adopted from the Hyksos, the New Kingdom pharaohs set the pace of this restless, energetic and aggressive age. They expelled the foreign overlords to make

Egypt a Bronze Age "superpower". They ventured where no pharaoh had gone before — to the watery and windy edges of the earth. They stood, together with so many ordinary Egyptians, at the threshold of a brave new world. They would map new geographies, both physical and psychological — terrains on the earth and mystic paths through the underworld. They would challenge old notions of gender, kingship and the nature of Egyptian religion itself.

Much of what we know about some areas of ancient Egypt is still based on conjecture and is uncertain because of the poor nature of our evidence. Our notions of what ancient Egyptians did, knew and believed are under perpetual discussion and revision. Egyptology can be a controversial subject. Present day Egyptologists are constantly making new discoveries which often overturn our knowledge and understanding. I have identified various Egyptologists whose contributions are recent and still under discussion, others whose work is established, and some whose discoveries have transformed Egyptology itself.

The world of the ancient Egyptians is fascinating, and grows even more so with every discovery made. Theirs was a civilisation in which the spiritual animated the physical, in which the concepts of the various levels of existence were at their most complex and sophisticated stage of development. In this book I have attempted to present something of the lives of the ancient Egyptians: their mystical beliefs, their everyday lives, their love for their land. It is my hope the reader, through this book, experiences a little of what it was like to be Egyptian during the New Kingdom era.

Note: Dates given for kings, for example, Thutmose III (c. 1505–1451 BC), refer to the period of their reigns.

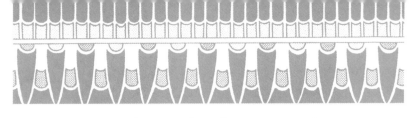

Gift of the Nile, Image of Heaven

➤ *Sunrise — the World Begins* ◆

One of the strangest objects uncovered by the English Egyptologist, Howard Carter, during the greatest archeological find of this century, was a sculpted wooden head of the boy king, Tutankhamun (*c*.1335–1326 BC), rising from an open lotus flower. Layered with plaster and then painted, it had begun to flake. The crown of the head was elongated and raised like a baby's at birth.

Here is the heart of Egyptian belief staring out at us, over three thousand years, wide-eyed and serene, through the flaking paint and plaster. The king has become the sun god, Re. He was released from the first flower of creation, the unfolding lotus on the primeval mound. This first hill appeared above the receding waters of chaos at the dawn of life on earth. The Egyptians called this moment the "first time", understanding their own origins extended back to this event. They called themselves the "Sun folk".

◀ *Wide-eyed Tutankhamun emerges from an opening lotus. This wooden statue of the boy king, found in his tomb, was designed to magically transform him into a god, Re, the Lord of Creation, blazing with supernatural light at the dawning of his afterlife.*

▲ *The world the New Kingdom Egyptians knew — from the cities of Thutmose III's distant victories in the north — Megiddo and Kadesh — to the difficult southern terrain of the Nile's Fourth Cataract where the river flowed from north to south along its great "S" bend. Egypt's modern capital, Cairo, lies near the Old Kingdom Pyramids of Giza.*

▲ *Shu, the god of air, tenderly and firmly raises his daughter, Nut, goddess of the sky from her brother, Geb, god of the earth. Both of Shu's arms are supported by the ram-headed Khnum, another creator god. It was every Egyptian's hope that the air (Shu) would open for him in an afterlife where Nut, as the sky, soared over him forever.*

⇒ The First Gods and the Creation ⇐

This vision of the world's beginning was a reflection of the Egyptians' experience of their own land. They saw it year after year as the Nile flood ebbed, leaving rich black silt studded with small ridges and hills. On an ancient hill, the "primeval mound", they believed that Atum, a form of the creator sun god, had stood alone. He sent his seed into the chaos, which brought the forces of air and moisture into being. The Egyptians called the air, the god Shu and moisture, the goddess Tefnut. They formed the first divine couple. The union of Shu and Tefnut then gave birth to the sky goddess Nut and the earth god Geb. Nut is often depicted naked, stretching over her brother-husband Geb. Their father Shu, standing between them, supports Nut above Geb as he lies on the ground — air rises to spread the sky away from the earth.

⇒ Egypt — Gift of the Nile ⇐

One of the most memorable descriptions of Egypt was penned by the Greek historian, Herodotus, two and a half thousand years ago. He called Egypt "the gift of the Nile". Indeed, in southern Egypt, with the

exception of sudden storms, it rarely rained. Egypt is a long, sun-drenched oasis, surrounded by a vast desert and watered by the river Nile on its way northward to meet the Mediterranean Sea. Of all the great rivers on earth, the Nile blessed its people with the most consistent and predictable cycle of seasons.

The waters of the Nile reached their lowest level in May. Then each year summer rains inundated east Africa's great lakes and mountain ranges. The effect of this distant southern drenching was evident as the river level slowly rose in late May to become a flood by late June. These waters were a gift. They came at the hottest time of the year, without dark clouds and rain, flooded the land for three months and left a deep carpet of black silt in their wake.

The Nile's flood cycle framed the Egyptians' sense of time. Unlike our four seasons, they divided the year into three seasons. Their New Year's Day was signalled by the ascent, just before dawn, of the bright star Sirius. Its rise heralded the annual flood, which is Egypt's first season, *Akhet*, the inundation season from July to October. The next four months saw the season of *Peret* when the land emerged from under the flood waters, ready for winter sowing. Between March and June during *Shemu*, the barley and emmer crops were harvested. It was a time of intense farming activity. Once the grains were collected and stored, the river level started to rise again.

▶ *Zigzagging blue lines stream down the plump body of the figure of the Nile. In his right hand he holds the hieroglyph,* renpet, *"year". Each rib represents one flood per year.*

▲ *The divine sisters of Osiris, Isis and Nephthys are present when the sun rises. Here the sun disc is raised by a pair of arms extending from the hieroglyph* ankh, *"life", mounted on the* djed *pillar ("stability and rebirth"), before these goddesses who played a crucial role in their brother's resurrection.*

This cyclical process profoundly impacted on the way Egyptians thought. They imagined the river as a well-fed, blue man. His head band and hand securely held upright palm ribs symbolising the length of the year, from flood to flood.

Each year the people of the Nile watched their land dissolve and disappear under the rising waters, only to see it re-emerge blanketed in dense fertile alluvium. This cycle of destruction and rebirth also shaped the character of the divine children of the sky and the earth, gods whose destinies were conditioned by the unique Egyptian environment and, who, in their turn, fashioned the nature of the Egyptian understanding of life on earth and an existence after death.

Osiris — the Green God of Regeneration

The cosmic union of Nut and Geb eventually gave birth to Osiris and Isis, Seth and Nephthys. Osiris, Geb's eldest son, ruled the world wisely. He brought to humankind the gifts of civilisation including agriculture. His jealous brother Seth planned to murder him, take the throne and Osiris' sister-wife, Isis. He tricked Osiris into lying in a superbly crafted chest. Once inside, the chest became Osiris' coffin. Seth and his henchmen sealed it, and cast it into the Nile. The fatal chest, adrift in the Mediterranean, beached itself at Byblos in Lebanon.

Grief stricken, Isis searched far and wide for her brother's corpse. Finally she came to Lebanon. There she found that a tamarisk tree had grown around Osiris' chest. The local king had heard of this marvellous tree. He ordered it cut down and installed in his palace as a column. Isis, using potent magic, secured Osiris' body and brought it back to Egypt.

According to one story, she turned herself into a kite, spreading her long shady wings over prone Osiris. The magic motion of her wings briefly breathed life back into Osiris and he impregnated her. The result of this union was Horus, the next rightful king of Egypt, his murdered father's heroic avenger.

This myth explained the transfer of power in the royal household: from the father, who died and became Osiris, Lord of the Dead, to his son who ascended the throne as Horus, Lord of the Living.

▶ *In this vignette from Nakht's* Book of the Dead, *the god of vegetation and resurrection, green-skinned Osiris, is enthroned in the company of the goddess of truth and order, Maat.*

➤ *Black Land, Red Land — Life-in-Death* ◄

In the life, death and resurrection of Osiris, the Egyptians also dramatised the confrontation between the forces of life and those of death. Green-skinned, tranquil, civilised Osiris is murdered by stormy, barbaric, red-haired, jealous Seth. Osiris stands for life, the great Egyptian oasis and peaceful agricultural order; Seth represents the wild, dangerous, sterile chaos of the desert.

The place where these opposing forces meet is starkly demarcated in the landscape. It is possible to stand with one foot on moist cultivated soil, the other on a dry barren wasteland. In the time of the pharaohs the Egyptians, with this absolute physical distinction under their own feet, simply called their land *Kemet*, the black land; the desert was *Deshert*, the red land. Here order met chaos.

They lived and worked in their fields, the black land. They buried their dead in the red land. But they had learnt from the Nile's miraculous flood cycle and from the Osiris myth that life always follows death. It is natural that Osiris is often portrayed in wall paintings with green face and hands, or shown lying in his human-shaped coffin with watered grain stalks rising from his funereal bed.

The Egyptians brought the vital power of the black land into their tombs in the red realm of death. In Tutankhamun's tomb an "Osiris bed", framing his distinctive silhouette in wood, was filled with Nile soil and sown with grain to sprout after the king's burial. The ceiling of Queen Nefertari's burial chamber was supported by columns painted with a *djed* pillar which is fashioned in the form of the tied sheaf of the harvest's first corn. Found in royal tombs both the Osiris bed and

◄ *This amulet, perhaps representing sheaves of grain bound around an upright pole or a simplified human spine, represents the hieroglyph,* djed. *It provided its owner with stability, durability and the power of rebirth.*

◀ *In Egypt today the line between the desert and the cultivated fields is still unmistakable. On one side is life and fertility, on the other death and the sterile sand — these have existed side by side for thousands of years, shaping the Egyptian landscape and imagination.*

the *djed* pillar embodied the forces of the resurrection of both Tutankhamun as the risen Osiris and as the upright enduring supports for the eternal survival of Queen Nefertari.

➤ *Survival of the Dead* ◄

Yet the Egyptian experience of the Red Land also instilled them with a sense of existence after death. Prehistoric burials have been found in the desert. The hot sterile sand dried out a corpse to such an extent that the deceased's flesh and bones, even down to hair and nails, remained perfectly preserved. The Egyptians began to wonder about what had filled and moved this empty physical shell. They gradually formulated the notion

◀ *Isis suckles her son Horus, protected by Egypt's northern marshes from the marauding Seth. Seth had killed Horus' father, Osiris, Isis' beloved brother. Isis taught young Horus magic. Eventually he would avenge his father's death.*

that the basic physiology of a human being co-exists with other subtle elements of being such as the *ka* or "lifeforce" which animated the body, the *khet;* and the *ba* or "spiritual manifestation", often depicted as a bird with a human head, released at death. These spiritual bodies initially were exclusive to the king, but later other Egyptian social classes claimed to possess them. Both the Lands, Black and Red, gave their inhabitants powerful intimations of a life beyond death, as echoed in the Osiris legend.

➤ *The Battle of Horus and Seth* ◄

Safe from Seth his father's assassin, Horus was born to Isis in the cover of Egypt's northern marshland thickets. Horus grew up there, aided by his mother's protective healing magic. Once a man, he challenged Seth for his rightful inheritance. When he took Seth before a tribunal of Egypt's chief gods, two of these, Shu and Thoth, supported Osiris' son. Overjoyed, Isis wanted the North Wind to relay the good news to Osiris in the netherworld. However, Re the president of the court sided with Seth.

In the prolonged struggle that followed, Horus suffered a horrific blow. Seth ripped out Horus' eye and tore it into bits, scattering it across the skies. Thoth came to Horus' aid, gathered most of the eye's pieces and restored the eye to Horus.

◄ *Seth, Lord of Chaos and Storms, is worshipped by Aapethi. Seth was hated for the vicious murder of his brother, Osiris, yet many Egyptians such as the pharaoh, Rameses II, revered him. Seth was the necessary counterpoint to harmony and order, a crucial element balancing the complex Egyptian universe.*

▶ *Thoth, the ibis-headed god of wisdom and writing who recorded the mysteries of the Egyptian gods and the deeds of humankind.*

Then Horus eventually avenged his father in a climactic episode represented by a beautiful statuette found in Tutankhamun's tomb. The young king, wearing the square crown of Lower Egypt, is poised on a papyrus boat with a raised harpoon in his right hand, a lasso in his left. Tutankhamun, as king of Egypt, is Horus, Lord of the Living. He is about to fatally spear Seth, lurking under the waters as a hippopotamus. Horus' opponent is not sculpted, out of fear of showing such a representation of evil. Here the living Horus, in the form of Tutankhamun, was in the act of defeating the forces of chaos and bringing the rightful balance of the world's god-given order back to Egypt. Horus had avenged his father and so ascended the throne. This is the essence of the Egyptian kingship.

⇒ *Horus — Bringer of Harmony* ⇐

The world each pharaoh ruled as the living Horus was *Kemet*, the Black Land, Egypt. It was divided into two distinct geographical areas: the Nile valley and delta. Over thousands of years the river had cut a long valley through hundreds of kilometres of limestone and sandstone plateau forcing its way north as Upper Egypt. About 200 kilometres (125 miles) from the Mediterranean Sea the Nile fanned out into a series of branches across an expanse of wide flat land known as Lower Egypt in the inverted shape of the Greek capital letter, delta.

This belief that the king of Egypt was the living manifestation of Horus is at least 1500 years older than the reign of Tutankhamun (*c.*1335–1326 BC). One of the earliest rulers of Egypt, Djer, had a stele,

◀ *Horus' solar eye pectoral is protected on either side by Nekhbet, the vulture goddess of Upper Egypt wearing a conical crown and Wadjet, the divine cobra with the square crown of Lower Egypt. These two Lands of Egypt, embodied in their patron goddesses, are united around Horus' solar eye.*

▶ *Horus' left lunar eye supports a dark disc rising from the crescent moon, borne by a celestial boat. A winged scarab beetle, symbol of the rising sun, lifts the heavenly boat aloft.*
In its hybrid talons the scarab clutches two shen *rings representing eternity and the lotus of Upper Egypt and Lower Egypt's papyrus. Horus balanced not only the two Lands of Egypt but also time itself.*

an upright stone slab, erected with Horus, the falcon god, perched above the tall frame containing the king's own name, symbolised by a snake. Djer's royal name rose above the stately crenellations of his panelled palace walls below.

Horus means "face" in Egyptian. They equated his face with the sky. They imagined his right eye as the sun, his left eye as the moon. In the battle with Seth, Horus lost an eye. Egyptians placed much faith in the protective and restorative power of the Eye of Horus, either as the waning and waxing of the left lunar eye or the completely restored right solar eye. By Tutankhamun's time these eyes were celebrated by two magnificent pieces of jewellery.

⋙ *Uniting the Two Lands of Egypt* ⋘

The rule of the living Horus was not always harmonious. Early in Egyptian history (over 5200 years ago) Upper and Lower Egypt were not united but in fierce conflict. Only when the Two Lands were united could the world begin for the Egyptians, who would be rightfully ruled by one king.

One of the major pieces of evidence for the unification of Upper and Lower Egypt under one ruler (*c.*3100 BC) is the Narmer Palette, a beautiful relief sculpture. Narmer, Egypt's first king, dominates the entire work. In the top register, symbols for this king's Horus name are placed in a central square above the outlines of palace walls. His name is surrounded by two human faces with the ears and horns of cows. These represent his consort Hathor, the goddess of love and fertility — "Hathor" means "the Mansion of Horus". A bearded Narmer stands wearing the tall white crown of Upper Egypt. Before him a defeated, near naked victim kneels. Narmer is about to smash his raised mace down on a peg, placed on the bare crown of his pacified opponent's head. Facing Narmer is a picture of a falcon with a human hand holding a rope tethered to the nose of a human head emerging from an oval. This oval forms the ground for a splay of papyrus plants. The falcon has landed on them.

These strange images are very early examples of Egyptian hieroglyphs or writing. They may be translated as "Horus dominates or overpowers the head of papyrus land, the king of Lower Egypt". Below Narmer's feet, in the bottom register, two other naked men lie in dejected poses of submission.

▶ *This piece known as the Narmer Palette commemorates the victories of King Narmer. Here, Narmer completes his triumph over Lower Egypt in the ritual execution of his defeated enemy. Many later kings imitated Narmer's action.*

◀ *Another way the Egyptians portrayed the Nile was as a pair of androgynous gods — one with the lotus of Upper Egypt and one with the papyrus of Lower Egypt. Here they bound these plants below the name of Rameses II. He had the Nile gods sculpted on this monument to proclaim his lordship of the Nile regions beyond Egypt at Abu Simbel.*

On the other side of this large palette, between the top two Hathors and the lowest register's image of the king's dominating force — represented by a bull standing on another naked foe, breaking apart a town's walls with his horns — are two registers signalling Narmer's achievements in uniting the Two Lands. In the second register Narmer, now with the red crown of Lower Egypt, inspects two macabre rows of his bound, decapitated enemies in the company of a male and a female official and a file of men holding standards, later known as "the followers of Horus". Below this gruesome scene of conquest, two mythic creatures are intertwined. They are held in balance by vigilant keepers holding ropes around their abnormally long necks. This is the consolidation of the conflict, maintaining the Two Lands in unity and harmony. Now the Horus Narmer is Lord of the Two Lands, wearer of the White and Red Crowns of Upper and Lower Egypt.

The Egyptians

Centuries later this binding of opposing forces was furthered when the king Senwosret I (*c.*1971–1928 BC) had Horus and Seth carved together on his throne base. Facing each other, their attention was centred on the hieroglyph for unification, *sema*, which is a pair of lungs with a tall trachea. Each god raised one foot to balance on one lung each, and tie the long stems of the plants of Upper and Lower Egypt around the trachea column. Seth grasped the lotus, Horus the papyrus. These ancient foes were reconciled in the active binding together of the Two Lands, such was the potency of the Union of Egypt.

Circuit the Two Lands, Ascend the Stairs — Djoser's Step Pyramid Complex

After the reigns of Narmer and Djer, the Egyptians entered their first great historical period, the Old Kingdom (*c.*2660–2125 BC). This was the period in which Egypt's rulers built a series of tombs which have

▼ *Looking south from Djoser's shrine court over the rims of local gods' shrines, his vast Step Pyramid looms majestically. As the Step Pyramid dominated the complex, Djoser from his throne at the head of this open court had the shrines of Egypt's gods lined up before him.*

21

▲ *These are the world's earliest stone columns. They were built in the northern court of Djoser's Step Pyramid complex to symbolise the stem and splay of three papyrus plants. They shyly emerge from the wall. Their builders were not yet confident enough to raise free standing columns.*

enthralled humankind ever since: the pyramids. The earliest surviving instance is the Step Pyramid Complex of King Djoser (*c.*2642–2622 BC), builder of the world's first stone monument, at Saqqara, west of the capital, Memphis.

Set on a North-South axis, the Step Pyramid Complex is enclosed in a vast complex of structures which reflect the unity of Upper and Lower Egypt: a colonnade with lotus and papyrus capitals (upper part of the column which widens out to support the beam above it); shrines of local northern and southern gods; a stone platform for a double throne with two small separate staircases at the head of the shrine court, where Djoser could sit as either king of Upper or Lower Egypt. There was also a large open air plaza where two pairs of semicircular stone structures were placed to represent the northern and southern limits of Egypt. Here, Djoser's regal spirit ran to claim his territory for all eternity, inside the high palace walls of his burial complex on the Nile's west bank.

Another sense dominated the complex. The Step Pyramid, itself a series of six tremendous bench-like steps raised one on top of the other to a

height of over 60 metres (200 ft), shadowed Djoser's earthly concerns as Lord of the Two Lands. This was the point of his transition from being the king of Upper and Lower Egypt as symbolised by the North-South axis to becoming one of the immortal beings of heaven. The king's eternal lifeforce could now ascend to heaven on his massive stone stairway.

The Sun on Earth — Khufu's Great Pyramid

Djoser's giant steps were later replaced during the reign of the next royal family of ancient Egypt, the Fourth Dynasty (*c.*2586–2470 BC), by a more ambitious plan for the pyramids. There is no direct evidence — no decrees or proclamations — but, as in Djoser's case, the pyramids' alignments and angles of incline reveal a cosmic purpose.

A true pyramid is a structure with smooth, straight ascending sides which imitate the slant of the sun's rays falling on the earth, in order to shape the world's "primeval mound", the place of creation.

▼ *These 4th Dynasty pyramids still soar above the horizon of Giza and our imaginations. From Menkaure's three queen's pyramids they rise up to Menkaure's, Khafre's and then to Khufu's. Khufu's pyramid is the greatest but Khafre's was built on higher ground and has much of its top casing still intact.*

After Sneferu's (*c.*2586–2561 BC) experiments in the construction of a true pyramid, his son Khufu (*c.*2561–2538 BC) built a massive true pyramid at the north-eastern edge of Giza's limestone plateau on the west bank of the Nile. It was called the Horizon of Khufu, *Khufu Akhet*. Khufu's name is linked to the place *Akhet* which means horizon. This is where earth meets sky, where in the west day becomes night and in the east night becomes day. This pyramid is a place of regeneration in the name of the king.

The Horizon of Khufu, it has been recently calculated by the Swedish Egyptologist, Sigvard Hellestam, was aligned to significant solar occurrences which marked crucial stages in the yearly cycle of regeneration. The great pyramid's base angles intersect the horizon at approximately 52 degrees. During its annual transit through the sky above Giza, the sun casts a shadow at noon from a vertical column of 52 degrees twice a year. These two occasions signalled a seasonal change in Egypt: when *Akhet*, the inundation season, became *Peret*, the growing season, and when *Peret* became *Shemu*, harvest.

While the hieroglyphic figures are different, the same word *Akhet* means both horizon and inundation season. This phonetic identification links Khufu's pyramid (the place of his burial and transformation from death to life), to the planting of seeds after the flood. Nile, earth, sun, pyramid and king are integral to the process of regeneration.

➤ *Image of Heaven* ◄
— *the Fourth Dynasty and the Stars*

The sky at night and Khufu's pyramid, it has long been speculated, also align at vital times of the year. Inside the pyramid there are what some Egyptologists call "ventilation shafts" rising from the structure's inner chambers.

Modern astronomers make mathematical adjustments, due to the slow "wobble" of the earth's axis, known as the precession of the equinoxes, to reposition the stars as they appeared thousands of years ago. It has been shown that for Khufu's Pyramid, over four and a half thousand years ago, at the crucial moment when Sirius, the night sky's brightest star, rose just before the sun at dawn to herald the Nile flood's rising water level at

▶*Inscribed on Unas' burial chamber below a carved star ceiling, are the world's earliest surviving religious writings – the* Pyramid Texts. *On the northern wall a series of offerings are listed. They are written there to magically sustain the king's spirit on his journey toward the northern stars.*

Giza, the top or king's chamber's southern ventilation shaft was oriented at the first star in Orion's Belt, Al Nitak, and the northern shaft at Alpha Draconis, which was the Pole Star during Khufu's distant epoch.

Writings known as the *Pyramid Texts*, humankind's earliest surviving religious literature, carved in hieroglyphics in later kings' burial chambers, equate Osiris with Orion, and Sirius with Osiris' consort Isis. While no final judgement has been made on these observations, the theories arising from it allow a tantalising, if cautious, glimpse into the Egyptian imagination where stars, pyramid, Nile and king are once again united in the destiny of the Two Lands.

⪢ *The Sphinx — Horus on the Horizon* ⪡

Khufu's son, Khafre (*c*.2530–2504 BC), built the second massive pyramid on the Giza plateau. Many scholars believe that he built the Sphinx, a colossal stone lion with a human head. It had Khafre's face and headdress. Later in Egyptian history, this proud guardian of the Giza pyramids was known as "Horus on the Horizon", *Hor em Akhet.*

The Sphinx's head could be seen between the two pyramid peaks of father and son. It appeared like the sun caught between these towering triangles, resembling the hieroglyph for the horizon, *Akhet*: the sun framed between two rolling hills. This solar connection is furthered by another heavenly event on the horizon. Each equinox the Sphinx's temple is in direct alignment with the setting sun sinking at the southern angle of incline of Khafre's pyramid. The Sphinx was dramatically caught in the middle. Its contours glowed, proclaiming the balance of the universe at the instant when the length of day equalled that of night. Then the sunlight streamed through the centre of the Sphinx temple's 24 columns: a blazing axis of geometric harmony — 12 hours of daylight; 12 hours of night.

▼ *Facing east the lion-bodied Sphinx guards the Giza pyramids. Its human head symbolising the regal sun is caught between the humanmade mountains of Menkaure's (left) and Khafre's pyramids, like the hieroglyph,* Akhet, *horizon — the sun rising or setting between two sloping mounds.*

➤ *Coronation in Heaven — the World is Remade* ◀

The capstone at the top of Amenemhet III's (*c.*1842–1797 BC) later pyramid also echoes the "first time", the beginning of the world. It was from a rise like this, known as the *benben*, that the winged sun creator god shone from this "primeval mound" to ejaculate creation's first male and female forces, air and moisture. This was also the place from which the wooden statue of Tutankhamun, carved as Re, would emerge magically on an opening lotus at the "first time".

The Egyptians believed that this "first time" would be recreated at the start of each new king's reign. The world entered chaos as the old king died. The Two Lands would fall apart. The new king would bring light and order to the shadowy, formless turmoil of death. At his coronation the world would be renewed. The falcon, Horus, took his rightful throne and the crowns of Upper and Lower Egypt. A New Year, a new era was announced as the Nile waters rose at the beginning of *Akhet*, and the king was crowned.

The world was now transformed as the forces shaping Egypt were harmonised in his divine kingship — the gods and humankind, the Nile and the Land, the Black Land and the Red Land, the Two Lands, male and female, heaven and earth, life and death, time and eternity.

▶ *At his own coronation Tutankhamun undoubtedly wore this spectacular jewelled pendant. With raised, outstretched wings of lapis lazuli, carnelian and blue glass, this golden falcon was Horus restored and triumphant over chaos. He rose with the carnelian sun disc, as this Horus grasped the hieroglyphs, ankh, for life and shen for eternity, in his soaring talons.*

The New Kingdom Begins —Lords of a Brave New World

➤ Heroic Egypt — One Against Many ◄

Sculpted in low relief, a colossal heroic figure strides across a vast wall at Amon Re's temple at Karnak in Upper Egypt. In his right hand he grasps a mace, like Egypt's first king on the Narmer palette.

This is where the resemblance to King Narmer stops. This figure is not holding a squat fatal peg to the bare crown of his lone victim's head like Narmer. He is gripping a long pole around which are bound the pathetic, gathered hair strands of his many enemies. They all kneel naked, raising their hands in submission. Their resigned, crowded faces sport foreign beards. This new king, Thutmose III, wearing the square crown of Lower Egypt, is poised above them.

Egypt had changed since the days of Narmer (c.3100 BC). It was, in this age of Thutmose III (c.1505–1451 BC), united, confident, energetic and aggressive on an imperial scale celebrated at a massive temple dedicated to a god, Amon-Re. Narmer would perhaps have only heard of this god as a shadowy force of darkness, Amon, the hidden one. Now Amon-Re was Egypt's chief deity. His son, Thutmose III, was about to smite Egypt's myriad enemies. It was an unmistakable message. The Egyptians stood alone, victorious over their enemies to the north into Asia, as portrayed on this wall, and to the south in Africa.

▲ *Looking north at the ruined Seventh Pylon at the Karnak temple of Amon-Re, with the tall columns of the Hypostyle Hall in the background to the north-west, a relief carving of Thutmose III on the western pylon (left) strides into action against Egypt's enemies. His power and victory protects this sacred precinct from evil forces.*

▼ *Below Thutmose III's feet are rows of crenellated ovals encompassing the hieroglyphic name of each foreign city conquered. A head emerged at the top of each oval with the arms bound behind the back of each city wall.*

➤ *The New Kingdom Begins* ◄ — *a Restlessness Emerges*

How did this change come about? How had the Pyramid Age of Egypt, the Old Kingdom, become so brash? It had appeared to be changeless; there was the harmony of heaven on earth, the gleaming peaks of the god kings; it was left undisturbed by the rest of the world. Now it was obsessed with military might and the slaughter and subjugation of foreign peoples.

A restlessness suffused the time of Thutmose III. He left Egypt on distant campaigns seventeen times during his reign. He did not build a pyramid. The divinely ordained flow of the Egyptian Nile, and the east to west transit of the sun, were not enough to keep him enthralled at home.

➤ *Decline and Renewal of Egyptian Power* ◄

The sunlit, starlit eternal Egyptian horizon had darkened long ago, shaken by the complex shades of human ambition, desire and weakness rising inside the Two Lands and beyond. Conspirators whispered in the palace corridors; knives were drawn against the king; great dynasties decayed; new men, far from the capital, demanded more independence and power; the exclusive royal right to an eternal life after death was challenged; the economy was exhausted. The Old Kingdom (*c.*2660–2125 BC) fell apart, the centralised power of the monarchy could not hold. Chaos reigned. The pyramids and nobles' tombs were ransacked. Life lost its meaning.

Lords from different parts of Egypt simultaneously claimed the throne of Horus. Slowly, as had happened in Narmer's days, a ruling family from Upper Egypt asserted its claim over the Two Lands. They founded what was later known as the Middle Kingdom (*c.*2040–1782 BC).

Writers strained to give Middle Kingdom life a new meaning. The efforts of generations to build and maintain great monuments to the everlasting memory of certain individuals now seemed useless. Even the tombs of the greatest thinkers and writers were gone. Only their words were immortal. Some contemplated and desired death. Life only offered the spectacle of the successes of evil men.

This was an age when literature flourished, fired by these anxieties, kindled by another dread. Once the realm of the afterlife was the secure realm of the king and his family, protected by his elaborate funerary rituals and architecture. Now that everyone had the right to an afterlife, the terrain of the next world was open to everyone's fears and doubts. It could become a nightmare world where people walked upside down and swallowed their own faeces. Some began to doubt if there really was an afterlife. The heartfelt strain of ruling these Two Lands was even etched across the sculpted faces of Middle Kingdom pharaohs.

⮞ *Arrival of the Hyksos — "A Blast from God"* ⮜

Late in the Middle Kingdom, Egypt experienced a slow infiltration of peoples from Syria-Palestine under the pressure of mounting migration movements in Western Asia. As the power of the Middle Kingdom's central government weakened, more foreigners crossed over the delta region. The leaders of these peoples were known as the Hyksos, "rulers of foreign places". They challenged the Egyptian dynasty for the double crown. The Hyksos made their capital in the eastern delta at Avaris, even taking the ancient capital of the Pyramid Age, Memphis. Native Egyptians still held Upper Egypt, centred on Thebes, but Apopi, a Hyksos king, had the Theban dynasty encircled. He had made an alliance with the Nubians below Egypt's southern boundary at the Nile's First Cataract.

The Egyptians had never been so humiliated in their long history. To demonstrate his power over the Egyptian king, the Hyksos king, Apopi, arrogantly complained to Seqenenre (*c.*1575 BC), that he could hear hippopotami in Seqenenre's Thebes — over seven hundred kilometres away. The distant creatures, it seemed, were keeping Apopi awake at night.

⮞ *Fighting the Hyksos* ⮜ — *Egypt Rises Toward Superpower Status*

Later Egyptian writers demonised the Hyksos, claiming they ruled without the gods, in particular, Re. Yet their kings adopted Egypt's religious practices and beliefs. They still used the royal title "Son of Re". Many Egyptians were content with their rule in the north.

▲ *A later ruler, King Seti I shows his son Rameses II their proud heritage. The long lines list the names of Egypt's kings, dynasty by dynasty, each inscribed in hieroglyphs and protected by an elongated vertical oval — the royal cartouche.*

They left Egypt with many technical advances. They introduced bronze, a harder, more durable metal than Egypt's familiar copper. Paradoxically, this enabled Egypt to finally take its place as a Bronze Age "superpower" once the Hyksos were expelled. They also spread the use of weapons such as the Kheperesh sword; the composite bow, made from wood, bone and sinew, with twice the range of earlier Egyptian bows; new bronze armour; the harnessed horse and chariot (Egypt owes its use of the wheel to the Hyksos); and a new style of fortress.

Beside military hardware they also improved the quality of Egyptian life. The Hyksos left Egypt with the olive and the pomegranate trees. Egyptian textiles benefited by the introduction of new machines producing wider fabrics.

The Egyptian encounter with these "rulers of foreign places" also left them unsure of their own place in the world. Before Hyksos infiltration

and dominance, the Egyptians were secure behind the protection of vast deserts and the Mediterranean Sea. Now they were vulnerable to invasion, humiliated. The psychological effect of this experience changed Egypt forever. In the fury of its counterattack against the Hyksos in the 1570's BC, Egypt reforged Hyksos war technology to create a new military state, unknown in earlier epochs of Egyptian history.

A terrible Egyptian glory was being born in the reconquest of the Two Lands. The new warrior pharaohs would conquer to the limits of the world to ensure Egypt was as safe as it had once been. In this era, known as the New Kingdom, Egyptian kings proclaimed for the first time that they now ventured abroad to extend the boundaries of Egypt. They would be obedient to this new imperative for generations to come.

➤ *Egyptian Counterattack* ◄ *— the Expulsion of the Hyksos*

A new anger now shaped the attitude of the Lord of Two Lands. His officials counselled that their slice of Egypt was prosperous. Pharaoh Kamose (c.1574–1570 BC), whose reign lasted only four years, was the last king of the Seventeenth Dynasty. He was not going to just sit there while he was surrounded by, as he vented his wrath, a mere Syrian and a "negro".

▼ *On this golden fan base Tutankhamun commands two pieces of Hyksos technology — horse-drawn chariot and composite bow — in pursuit of fleeing ostriches. Many bows were found in his tomb.*

They had no right to claim any part of the Two Lands. An Egyptian must rule Egypt. There was to be only one "ruler" — Kamose, son of Seqenenre.

He ferociously set out to rid the Hyksos' supporters inside his own Egypt, then against their southern allies, the Nubians. He campaigned against the Hyksos king, Apopi, in the northern Hyksos capital, Avaris. Kamose died without taking Avaris.

Ahmose (*c.*1570–1547), son of Seqenenre, half-brother of Kamose and first king of the Eighteenth Dynasty and the New Kingdom, was too young to attack the Hyksos immediately. His grandmother Tetisheri, and then his mother Queen Ahhotep II were his regents, governing the Two Lands in his place. When he was old enough he took Egypt's forces

▼ *This pectoral was probably worn at his coronation by Ahmose and represents the "Baptism of the King". The gods Re and Amon-Re, flanking Ahmose, pour purifying cascades of water around the king as they all journey through heaven on the sun boat.*

back up against the Hyksos at Avaris. One of his loyal troops, a commoner, also called Ahmose (a marine who served under Seqenenre), wrote that he followed King Ahmose's chariot on foot and fought at Avaris bravely.

There is even a hint that the massive volcanic eruption of Thera (now known as Santorini) spewed across the Mediterranean towards Egypt's delta. The tephra fallout could have been read by the Hyksos as a sign that the gods were withdrawing their support from the Hyksos. A new era was signalled in the skies.

Once Avaris was captured, Ahmose attacked Sharuhen in Palestine and ventured beyond Egypt's traditional limits. This set a pattern for

▼ *Part of Nubia's resources — bound warriors, a mother and her children as well as livestock — file into Egypt.*

▲ *Egyptian power in Nubia was asserted by these colossal statues of Rameses II carved into the vast cliff face at Abu Simbel. This was a spectacular reminder to the Nubians of the supernatural identity of their lord and master.*

his successors. The boundary of Egypt was being extended in pursuit of these aliens. The Sharuhen siege lasted a long time. With Sharuhen's fall there was a further foray into Hyksos territory. The Hyksos were cast out. Egypt was set for further expansion.

Both Ahmose and his successor, Amenhotep I, turned their energies south to Nubia. The younger king started a colonisation program beyond the Second Cataract of the Nile. He appointed a special commander for this region, "the King's Son of Kush". Nubia's natural resources were to be exploited for the imperial cause — gold, silver, amethyst, ivory, ebony, cereal crops, perfumes, domestic and wild animals.

➤ *A Brave New World* ◄
— Beyond the Boundaries of the Two Lands

Further north new powers were forcing their way into Syria. The Hittites destroyed the old domain of Yamkhad in northern Syria, whose capital was Aleppo, creating a power vacuum in the wake of its disappearance. Another presence to the east, the Mitanni, began to

assert itself over the neutralised northern reaches of Syria and the Upper Euphrates. A confident, liberated Egypt, flushed with success, enriched by its exploitation of Nubia, could not but be drawn northward into this power vacuum.

A new pharaoh came to the throne, apparently unrelated to Amenhotep I (*c*.1552–1525 BC), eager to follow in the victorious footsteps of his predecessors and prove himself a rightful "son of Amon-Re" — Thutmose I (*c*.1525–1519 BC).

Very soon Thutmose I led Egyptian forces into places "where no wearer of the double crown" had ever ventured, into brave new worlds where nature obeyed unEgyptian rules. He and his men negotiated the Nile's disorienting north to south flow in the treacherous rocky waters at the Fourth Cataract. Here what had been in Egypt the west bank twisted — as the Egyptians continued their march northward up its "S" bend beyond the Third Cataract — to become the "east" bank, place of the sunrise.

▼ *The message of Egypt's subjugation of Nubia was further emphasised by Egypt's victories in the north represented by papyrus-bound captives, perhaps a Hittite (left) and a Syrian.*

Here the Nile flood was dreaded. Thutmose I's men needed a low water which exposed a chain of islands and much needed shorelines for their infantry to advance and to carry their boats upstream.

Even the wind was unEgyptian. Its northern gusts buffeted the soldiers' progress against the stream. In Egypt the prevailing wind blows against the current, driving a sailing boat up the Nile. Here, in the remote south, both river and wind conspired against the soldiers. Victorious finally against the rebellious Nubians, they stood at the windy edge of their world, hundreds of kilometres further than any Egyptian king had gone before. To mark the extended boundary, Thutmose I raised a stele.

Later, in what was the climax of his expedition northward into Syria, along the Orontes valley, he did the same on the east bank of the Euphrates River. Here, on this northern river's "Great Bend" was another waterway which contradicted Egyptian experience, by flowing north to south. They called this mighty stretch of water the "inverted river". Thutmose I had crossed the great waters of the world's northern limit. His stele, the presence of his undefeated army and his double crown, however briefly, gave the great powers of the region notice that Egypt was now a power to be reckoned with.

➤ *Thutmose I* ◄
— *Heroic Journeyer to the Ends of the World*

Egypt had now entered an age unparalleled in its history. Thutmose I erected another stele at Tombos island, just beyond the Third Cataract, to celebrate his successes. It is fired with a new destiny unfolding for Egypt. Thutmose I's journeys were unprecedented. He stood alone in Egyptian experience. Only the mythic kings of prehistoric legend have known the worlds Thutmose I had seen. This was a geography which Djoser, dashing around his territorial markers eternally enclosed by Saqqara's high walls, could never have known. The distant winds and waters at the world's limits began to beckon the Egyptians beyond the Two Lands. A young king, grandson of Thutmose I, was to fulfil the promise of this new destiny now driving the Egyptians beyond the security and harmony of the Nile.

➤ *Thutmose III, Warrior Pharaoh* ◄
— *Victory at Megiddo*

The promise of Egypt's new destiny was not fulfilled until after the reign of his son, Thutmose II. The Mitannian kingdom began to stake its claim to the north. When the young King, Thutmose III (*c.*1505–1451), grandson of Thutmose I, finally assumed sole power in Egypt, he struck out for Palestine "to overthrow that wretched enemy, to extend the boundaries of Egypt".

The Mitannian king confronted Egypt with a network of northern states under his sway and a strong coalition of southern Syrian and Palestinian cities sympathetic to him in their opposition to Egypt in about 1482 BC.

▶ *The athletic, bare-chested bust of the warrior pharoah, Thutmose III, like his grandfather, Thutmose I, gazes into the distance with alert-eyed confidence and authority. Thutmose III was Egypty's most successful king and general — pharoah as hero.*

Thutmose III marched north to meet this antagonistic alliance. He encountered them as they gathered at Megiddo (in present day Israel). Whether they were already together there, or had just formed up once news of Thutmose III's advance had become known is uncertain.

Like Kamose, Thutmose III had to deal with a chorus of cautious advisers. At his war council he showed his heroism. His council advised that he take his army along a longer, wider, safer route to the city. Thutmose III swore that, as he was the beloved favourite of Amon-Re, he would take the shortest, most dangerous narrow way to Megiddo, the Aruna Road. His horses and troops would have to approach Megiddo in single file. They would be vulnerable to being caught, and picked off one by one. But he would not be seen as a coward.

Amon did favour him. The enemy had not guarded the Aruna Road. The Egyptian army was able, safely and rapidly, to assume their battle formations out in the plain before the battle. Then they attacked. The enemy was unprepared. They fell apart before the Egyptians' decisive blow, led by their lord. Egyptian order overpowered foreign chaos. The people of Megiddo panicked. They shut their city gates on their own forces who had to be grappled over Megiddo's wall by the threads of their own clothes.

Yet the Egyptian army let Thutmose III down. They could have seized the opportunity and taken the city immediately. But they began to loot. The opportunity lost, Thutmose III had to settle for a long seven month siege. Even then he made a heroic virtue out of a disappointing necessity, naming the siege wall before Megiddo — "Menkhepere (Thutmose III): Encircler of Asiatics".

The Egyptian war machine is centred on the king. He is the attacker with nowhere safe to flee, unlike his enemies. He is the lone besieger holding the fate of the many in his hands, as he claimed on the Karnak wall: "the capture of Megiddo is the capture of a thousand towns". Once taken, Megiddo, with many coalition princes inside, opened the way for Thutmose III to secure the other Syrian-Palestinian cities united against him. The Mitannian king had lost a vital buffer zone.

▲ *Sculpted onto the wall of Horemheb's tomb, Syrian families are led toward the victorious general, Horemheb, who is shown further along the wall being showered with rewards from his king, Tutankhamun. The bearded captive in the centre has his wrists bound by a manacle.*

➤ *Egypt and the Mitanni* ◄
— *a Clash of Bronze Age "Superpowers"*

Thutmose III closed in. Ten years after Megiddo, he led his army from Byblos in Lebanon, equipped with pre-fabricated boats loaded in ox-carts across rugged terrain where it snowed in winter, through torrential streams and dense forests; another unEgyptian landscape to negotiate. However, Thutmose III had command of the logistics necessary to conquer this new world. After a series of tough encounters, Thutmose III pursued the Mitanni all the way to Carchemesh by the Euphrates. They hoped the great river would save them. They had not counted on Thutmose III's pre-fabricated overland navy. They shied away from a set battle with the formidable Egyptians, melting away before pharaoh. Their terrified ruler ran to a remote place. Many hid in caves.

➤ *Egypt Triumphant* ◄

A proud Thutmose III, emulating his grandfather's achievement, set up a stele on the Euphrates shore. Now, from beyond the limits of the Egyptian world, the great powers of the age took notice of Thutmose III's triumph. The Hittites, the Assyrians and Babylonians sent exotic presents to pharaoh with respect and appreciation.

Thutmose III celebrated his success, imitating his grandfather again, with an elephant hunt on the Niy marshlands of the Orontes River. There he confronted one hundred and twenty elephants. Pharaoh now subdued these wild beasts, complementing his control of the region, human and animal.

Another symbolic gesture of his mastery were the number of exotic animals and plants from the north which were copied and then later sculpted on the walls of his Festival Hall in the Temple of Amon-Re at Karnak. Thutmose III had descriptions of his exploits carved onto other walls near the temple's inner sanctum.

News of his triumphs went further south. They were inscribed in a temple at the other boundary of his extended realm on Gebel el Barkal, a mountain sacred to Amon-Re, deep in Nubia, by the Nile's windy Fourth Cataract. Now the achievements of his rule resounded from one distant boundary to another: "All the sun encircles is in my grip".

▲ *A detail of the unEgyptian animals and plants carved into the "Botanical Garden" walls of Thutmose III's Festival Hall at Karnak. Here the god of empire, Amon-Re, was celebrated for bringing the flora and fauna of the entire world, not just Egypt, into being.*

➤ *And All the King's Men* ◄

Despite the Thutmoside epic claims of the king securing victory after victory, it is obvious they were supported and, on occasion, saved by their brave and loyal troops. In the New Kingdom, for the first time in Egyptian history, there was a professional standing army. It was composed of men, proud of their career and the triumph of their acts and actions. Amenemhab, a soldier who fought under Thutmose III in the north, was rewarded for his bravery in battle with silver and gold.

➤ *The Spoils of Conquest* ◄

Egypt was enriched by the tribute and taxes which it gathered from the northern and southern wings of its domain. On the tomb wall of Rekhmire, Thutmose III's top government official, a troop of Nubians bring a giraffe, long-horned cattle, dogs and a monkey, while the Syrians contribute a panther, an elephant and horses. Records of the

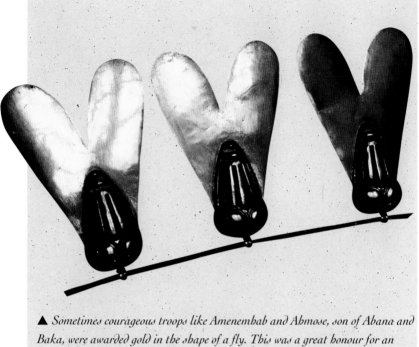

▲ *Sometimes courageous troops like Amenemhab and Ahmose, son of Abana and Baka, were awarded gold in the shape of a fly. This was a great honour for an Egyptian soldier. The fly represented a restless persistent being. This energy characterised Egypt under the New Kingdom warrior pharoahs.*

"tribute" from foreign lands show that nations unconquered by the Egyptians still thought enough of Egypt's power and prestige, despite the Egyptian claims that it was tribute, to present Thutmose with lavish gifts. In Rekhmire's tomb, men from unconquered Crete offer gold, copper, vases, daggers, necklaces and ivory tusks.

➤ *Order Out of Chaos* ◄

In battle foreigners are portrayed as a frenzied mass of confusion and panic. When they come before the Egyptians they are pacified and portrayed in orderly registers in single line, either holding tribute or gifts for the masters of their world or as bound by the Lotus and the Papyrus, the flowers of Upper and Lower Egypt. Here the fairer Syrians

◀ *A pair of sandal soles were painted at the base of many Egyptian coffins. Sometimes figures of bound foreigners were represented on Egyptian soles. With each step an Egyptian took in the afterlife, his feet, first left then right, crushed an enemy of Egypt — Syrian, Nubian — forever and ever. They imagined they controlled an everlasting empire.*

are counterpoised with the black Nubians. As the Lord of the Two Lands tied Southern and Northern Egypt together, now Syria-Palestine was knotted into the imperial fabric with Nubia.

Here Pharaoh brings order out of chaos. The chaotic behaviour of the foreigners is set row upon row in Egyptian order. This concept of order was personified as the goddess of Truth and Order, Maat. Pharaoh's task was to bring *maat* — the concept of truth, balance and order — to the world and to extend Egypt's boundaries. Maat in return protected and blessed pharaoh on his Throne of the Two Lands, Lord of a brave new world, bordered by wind and water, celebrated by his Five Great Names.

➤ *The Five Great Names of Pharaoh* ◄

Each New Kingdom pharaoh had Five Great Names. They started with *Horus*, the king was the living reincarnation of Horus; *Two Ladies*, he was protected by Nekhbet and Wadjet, the vulture and cobra goddesses of Upper and Lower Egypt; *Gold Horus*, perhaps re-emphasising Horus' divinity because the gods had golden flesh; *Lord of the Two Lands*, ruler of Upper and Lower Egypt; and *Son of Re*, his father is the Sun God, Re.

These last two names are written inside a cartouche. It is an oval of cord, originally the hieroglyph, *shen*, symbol of eternity and protection, but then elongated to hold these two names, protecting him forever.

▼ *The most valuable find in Egypt was the key to Egyptian hieroglyphs — the Rosetta Stone. Here, a later king's ascent to the throne was recorded in Egyptian hieroglyphs, demotic (a more simplified shorthand style of Egyptian writing) as well as Greek. Egyptian hieroglyphs have been carved just above the demotic script. One name of the king is written inside a horizontal cartouche. It is introduced by the hieroglyphs — the sedge plant and the bee — representing his lordship over Upper and Lower Egypt.*

▲ *At the distant reaches of his empire such as Abu Simbel rises a larger than life statue of Queen Nefertari, only to be dwarfed by the colossal dimensions of her husband, the king, Rameses II.*

By the Sunlit, Starlit Nile

➤— Safe Again —◄

New Kingdom Egyptian civilisation (*c*.1570–1070 BC) flourished as an oasis, protected by the vast deserts, the Mediterranean Sea, and now, by Pharaoh's army and navy, in harmony with the Nile's seasons and the sky, where the dawn ascent of Sirius announced the Nile flood. Pharaoh ruled to ensure the continuity of this truth, order and balance: *maat*. The New Kingdom Egyptians could now safely live, work and play by the starlit, sunlit Nile.

▲ *Hidden from the unrelenting Egyptian sun a shady oasis of palm trees, grass and water provides a gentle refuge for the Egyptian people.*

⋙ A Place of Flowers and Trees — an Egyptian Idyll ⋘

The ideal spot for an Egyptian was a space alive with flowers and trees. There she or he could enjoy the cool shade, the river breezes and the flowers' fragrance. Rameses III founded a new northern town, lining it with mighty vineyards; lanes shaded by arching branches laden with delicious fruit; a sacred avenue, ablaze with flowers of every nation, and with as many lotus and papyrus blooms as there are stars in the sky.

The word for a garland of flowers in Egyptian is *ankh*. It also means life. This identity encapsulates the vivid connection between the natural, human and divine worlds. The gods were constantly portrayed carrying the *ankh* hieroglyph. It resonated with the idea of life eternal. Naturally Egyptians buried their dead with bouquets of flowers.

The rich imitated their pharaoh. Often they constructed their own homes in the seclusion of high walls with rows of palm, sycamore, fig and other fruit trees, as well as vines, framing large pools of water, and an abundance of flowers.

⋙ Egyptian Marriage ⋘

The heartfelt romance of Egyptian love poetry reveals that Egyptian marriages were not always coldly arranged by the couple's families. Many statues of married couples reveal a genuine affection for each other.

Egyptians married at a young age. Twenty was a suitable age for a man. The woman was often as young as fourteen years old. Despite the fact that in formal documents husband and wife were known as "brother" and "sister", the royal practice of a brother marrying his sister was a rarity in the rest of Egyptian society.

Getting married was uncomplicated. No state ceremony or temple ritual was needed. The couple simply moved in together, with the marriage contract settled. This agreement recognised the rights of both parties to a marriage. Here women had equal rights to men when it came to the possession and use of property.

In the event of a divorce, it was as simple to get as it was to marry. If the man was at fault, the woman was entitled to at least a third of the settlement. If the breakdown was the woman's fault she could still expect some form of maintenance from her ex-husband.

▲ *This wall painting portrays Inherkhau and his wife seated side by side, joyfully listening to the song of a blind harpist. Marriage in ancient Egypt was an uncomplicated affair.*

➤ Childbirth ◄

Men and women married to have children, to continue the family line. A mother-to-be may have had her own series of pregnancy tests. Using their commonsense, ancient Egyptians checked her pulse rate, watched the colour of her eyes, her complexion, and observed the frequency of her vomiting. Magic practice also played its part. If a woman passed water over cloth covering wheat and barley and the barley sprouted, she would deliver a boy; if wheat emerged, a girl; no shoots, no child.

As the foetus grew the mother may have dipped her finger into an oil container, and then massaged herself to ease her discomfort and lessen the likelihood of stretchmarks.

The child might have been born in a confinement pavilion, with papyrus stem columns laced with winding grapevines or the twisting tendrils of a trumpeting convolvulus. It was set up, just before confinement, outside the house, in the garden or on the roof. Among

the workers' families at Deir el Medina this vital time would have been spent in the front room of the house, where the family chapel with offering niches and ancestral busts had been built.

The dwarf god, Bes, and the hippopotamus goddess, Thoeris, were painted on the wall to protect mother and child. A brick structure was set up inside the private chapel. It may have formed a birthing bed. This may have been the place for the apotropaic wand to ward off demons who may threaten the mother during childbirth. Spells were said over the bricks on which the mother squatted for the baby to be born. One spell called on Horus to save the woman in labour, and on Hathor, goddess of love and fertility, to assist the woman with the healing touch of a magic amulet.

This spell was uttered four times over a magic amulet of Bes. It was placed on the mother's forehead during a difficult and dangerous labour.

▼ *Bes, an ugly yet benevolent dwarf-god, sports a lion's mane and ears to frame a broad frown. His grotesque face was meant to frighten away evil spirits, especially those which would endanger a woman in childbirth.*

◆ An Egyptian Childhood ◆

Egyptian life made great demands on everyone. The sense of having a childhood before entering school or work was not long. But we have archeological evidence of toys and dolls. There was also participation in games and sports. Soon most young Egyptians were apprenticed into the family trade. A rare few were able to go to school.

◆ School for Scribes ◆

At school the young scribe, sometime between five and ten years old, depending on his maturity and readiness, learnt by heart the hieroglyphic signs, word after word, phrase after phrase. *Kemit* or "Summary" was the simple text young scribes used to learn the Egyptian language and script. As they grew up they were taught

◀ *Being sculpted as a scribe endowed an Egyptian with wisdom and learning. Many of Egypt's most celebrated sages such as Amenhotep, son of Hapu, were portrayed seated with their open papyrus scroll spread across their crossed legs in the process of writing.*

how vile other occupations were: the smith, slaving at his furnace, had fingers like a crocodile's claws; or the stone mason, exposed to the searing elements, toils through the years with aching loins and weary limbs.

The life of a scribe was, according to this *Satire of the Trades*, a pleasant existence. He has power over everyone. His ability to read and write is more valuable than food, drink, clothes or ointment, even a tomb for the afterlife.

If a scribe joined the civil service, it was claimed, he did not have to pay taxes. In an advanced text, *Miscellany*, Raia the scribe built himself an idyllic house and garden. Being a scribe had its material comforts. However, some students, still dissatisfied, bucked the system. Their misbehaviour was judged severely. They were put in the stocks. They were treated like prisoners.

➤ *School Houses* ◄

In the New Kingdom, schools existed in at least two locations: at the back of Rameses II's mortuary temple, the Ramesseum, and in the temple of Mut, Amon-Re's wife. There may have been one in the royal tomb builders' village, Deir el Medina in Western Thebes. It educated the workers' children. They needed to read and write. They had to copy the sacred texts of the royal Books of the Netherworld onto the walls of kings' and queens' tombs, organise the day to day operation of the working gangs, and make requests and complaints to their superiors in Eastern Thebes.

Their children's early education seems to have taken place in the Ramesseum, or later in Rameses III's mortuary temple, Medinet Habu. Afterwards they would have been assigned to learn their literate craft with an older male — a neighbour perhaps, father or uncle.

▶ *Essential equipment for an Egyptian scribe — even a king. Tutankhamun's ivory palette with writing reeds and two round containers with separate colour cakes for different inks — red and blue-black.*

Their literacy education even extended to the classics of Egyptian literature, like the Middle Kingdom's *Tale of Sinuhe*. A large stone has been found there with a copy of Sinuhe's adventures beyond Egypt.

We do have written references to a village school, but no archeological evidence of an actual school house has yet been located in the village precinct. Since the village area was littered with many literary ostraca (limestone flakes or broken pottery sherds) one could assume that schooling occurred outside in the open Egyptian air, with

▼ *Copied from an earlier mathematical text the Rhind papyrus reveals that the Egyptians did not depend so much on mathematical theory, but trusted in practical solutions to a series of problems.*

students sitting in the traditional scribal manner, their legs crossed at the ankles, and their writing material laid across their lap. This writing board may have taken the form of a plastered piece of wood. Its brushed ink could be erased with a wipe.

⋙ *Women and Writing* ⋘

Most scribes were destined to work in the Egyptian civil service. There were no places for women in this bureaucracy. There were a few posts in the priesthood for women but not as scribes. The Egyptian language reveals the male domination of the writing profession. The feminine form of scribe indicated someone who painted (made up) her mistress.

There is, however, some evidence that women were literate. At Deir el Medina, thousands of ostraca (limestone flakes) were used for writing. Many were addressed to and written by women. In some noble women's tomb paintings there is evidence in the form of a writing scroll. Clearly these were part of some women's everyday lives. They could read and write. They may have been educated simply as part of their high social standing.

▶ *With a face as rough as the surface of this limestone flake a big, bald workman from Deir el Medina grins as he wields his mallet and chisel. Many workers like this formed gangs which cut into the limestone depths of the Valley of the Kings.*

➤ *Life on the Black and Red Lands* ◄

Most Egyptians were unable to read and write. They formed the wide base of the New Kingdom's social pyramid where the pharaoh, his family, the nobles and high officials and priests were at the top; the middle section being taken by lower priests, artists and soldiers, followed by the peasant farmers who worked the fertile tracts of the black land.

Most Egyptians lived and died working on the rich fertile land, laced with canals to further the water's flow. Their working existence was framed by the rise and fall of the Nile. After the annual flood (the season of *Akhet*) farmers plugged the canals to hold the vital water longer. They planted seeds for their crops by hand. Their pigs and goats trampled the seeds into the silt during the season of *Peret*. The farmers then worked hard to bring in the harvest during *Shemu*. The produce of every Egyptian farmer, usually working on Pharaoh's or the temple's land, was strictly audited by supervising scribes. Sometimes the farmer could be punished for not meeting his required amount of grain. He was beaten for his troubles.

Beneath the farmers were all the foreign slaves brought into Egypt as part of the spoils of Pharaoh's victories. They worked on the royal building programs, erecting the mighty pylons and obelisks to the conquering gods of Egypt, and in the harsh mines and quarries in the desert. Their living conditions must have been horrendous in the desolate quarries. They worked all day under relentless, blinding sunlight. With their primitive tools, they had to cut through impenetrable granite boulders. So much of the splendours of Egypt's temples were created at the cost of thousands of lives; miseries unwitnessed by the privileged worshippers. However, it must be remembered that this suffering was not on the scale of other civilisations like Assyria, Babylon or Rome.

▶ *Once the tomb walls had been rendered smooth the village artists created beautiful portraits of their kings and queens encountering the gods in the afterlife. Rameses II's graceful queen, Nefertari, raises two pots in a devout offering gesture.*

➤ *"The Place of Truth"* ◄
— *a Working Week in the Valley of the Kings*

The pharaohs did not rely on slave labour for their beautiful rock-cut tombs in the Valley of the Kings. They created a village whose inhabitants worked on their tombs, who were paid in the form of housing, food and clothing from the royal treasury. The place where they lived is now called Deir el Medina, originally known as "The Place of Truth" during the New Kingdom. Its men were organised into two gangs, like sailors on a ship, the "left" and the "right". In this military formation they systematically cut their way into the limestone cliff face of the "Great Place", the Valley of the Kings. There they worked an eight hour shift with a morning and an afternoon session. Their working week lasted ten days. They were given one day off.

➤ *Royal Work, Fringe Benefits* ◄

The workers' superiors often allowed their free day to stretch across a couple more days into a "long weekend". The work force had enough free time to work for themselves and earn a little more than the wages Pharaoh provided in food and shelter. They indulged in what we would call "moonlighting". They could, as skilled artisans, hire out their talents. Scribes could draw up letters, prepare contracts, inscribe chapters and scenes from *The Book of The Dead* on tomb walls and papyri or have their brushes paint spells and other sacred writings on coffins. Carpenters constructed furniture and coffins. Sculptors created prayer stelae and family statues. Painters decorated coffins and tombs.

◄ *Sennedjem and his wife plough the "Field of Reeds". The Egyptians projected their experience of their land and river into a perfected version of vast harvests and fields without snakes in a plentiful life after death.*

◀ *Menna (middle register, centre left), overseer of state lands, is offered wine as he shelters in a papyrus kiosk. Before him, workers winnow the threshed harvest, tossing it in the air to separate the grain from the chaff.*

By a system of bartering goods — one pig, two goats, two sycamore logs and an agreed amount of copper could buy one coffin — the workers were able to live well above the basic rations of ordinary Egyptians. However, it was never enough to match a noble's lifestyle or even afford a royal official's funeral. Despite the fact that some owned tracts of land, livestock and even possessed slaves in their households, the workers could not ascend from their unique place on the Egyptian social pyramid.

➤ Food Production — the Blessings of Osiris ◀

The main crops were barley and a variety of wheats, including emmer. These formed the staple ingredients of an ordinary Egyptian's diet — bread and beer. In the New Kingdom, the *shaduf*, a manually operated device which lifted water from the Nile up onto the dry land, enabled Egyptians to spread their use of water. Together with the rich soil, it helped the Egyptians, if they needed, to grow a second crop during their hot months.

Vegetables — garlic, beans, onions, radishes, cucumbers, peas and lettuce — were grown apart from the wheat and barley in compact square plots. Wine from pressed grapes were produced for Egypt's upper classes. Other fruits such as dates (used to flavour the beer), figs, pomegranates were available to the population, especially during festival days.

▲ *Grape pickers at work under a vault of vines heavy with bunches of grapes. These were then taken to the press and crushed under foot, eventually to be stored in jars inscribed with the date when they were finally sealed.*

Wild and domesticated bees produced Egypt's principal sweetener, honey. Honey was mixed with bread to make cakes. It also sweetened the thick Egyptian beer, along with dates. These two substances accelerated the process of fermentation after water was added to the partly baked cakes. They were eventually dissolved. The resulting mixture was left to ferment in a warm area.

➣ *Meat Production and Distribution* ➤ *— Social Class and Festivals*

Cattle comprised Egypt's most common livestock. Long- and short-horned varieties as well as the humped Brahminy bull grazed on the wide New Kingdom temple and royal estates. They were not only raised to provide meat but also for their milk, their physical strength to carry and pull, and their sacred use as sacrifices.

▲ *Long- and short-horned as well as Brahminy cattle are herded for inspection. The artist has paid careful attention to the colour and detail of each animal being brought before the inspecting scribes.*

Earlier attempts to domesticate the antelope and hyena had failed. Along with rabbits and other wild animals, they provided some meat for the poor as well as sport for the nobles' hunting parties. Domesticated animals such as goats and pigs were tended for their meat, as were ducks, geese and, from the New Kingdom, chickens which were used as well for their eggs. Besides the occasional forage in the desert wilderness ordinary Egyptians could eat some meat at festivals.

⋟ *Fish — Diet and Taboo* ⋞

Salted fish formed part of the Deir el Medina workers' wage rations, while poorer people could supplement their diet with Nile or Mediterranean fish which were plentiful. Fish had varying religious associations. In one version of the Osiris legend, when he was cut into

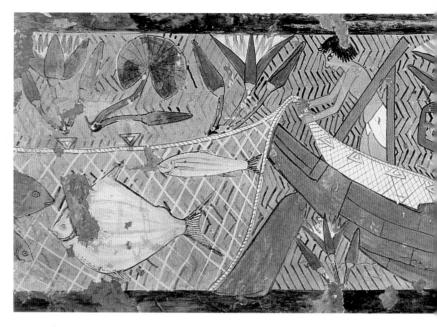

pieces by Seth his severed penis was swallowed by a fish, sometimes identified as the Oxyrynchus fish. In the tomb of a Deir el Medina worker, Kabekhnet, Anubis the jackal-headed god of the dead is pictured embalming a fish. The goddess Hatmehit, leader of the fishes, was worshipped at her holy city, Mendes, in the Egyptian Delta.

The sacred aspects of some fish made them forbidden eating in some districts of Egypt. Further downstream or upstream, people in places without these religious beliefs would think nothing of consuming these fish. This variation in belief would cause tension between some of Egypt's settlements.

➤ *Clothing and Textiles* ◄

One of the by-products of Egyptian agriculture was flax. Its fibres formed the threads of Egypt's most important woven fabric — linen — a light, cool material.

The tomb of Kha and Meryt from Deir el Medina, one of the few intact tombs excavated in Egypt, stored twenty six shirts and fifty loincloths, some of which could have been worn in the fields or on

▲ *The Nile provided a rich food resource for the population. This painting depicts fishermen at work on board a small boat. One hauls in the net's catch.*

construction sites. There were also thicker tunics for the winter. Clothing from Tutankhamun's tomb reveal golden threads laced through some of his clothes. A kilt of compressed coloured beads was also found there.

Besides these archeological discoveries, statues and wall paintings further expand our knowledge of Egyptian dress. Most men wore a kilt. It extended from the waist to just above the knee. Women wore, according to the evidence of Egyptian art, tight dresses covering their breasts and reaching their ankles.

The New Kingdom saw a more complicated and sophisticated sense of dress, driven by fashion, and distinguished by a swathe of pleats and fringes. Over a short kilt men wore a densely pleated long skirt, brought together at the hips, where a pleated apron, covered by a fringed sash, reached out past the knees. Above the waist they wore a linen tunic with pleated sleeves.

Women continued to wear their tight skirts, but in the New Kingdom, feminine dress sense came into its own. Then they wore over the skirt a fringed robe, made of seamless cloth with much pleating. It was folded around the waist, raised over the shoulders, and finally knotted under the breasts to secure the dress.

▼ *Detail from the lid of a casket found in Tutankhamun's tomb. With a layered wig, Tutankhamun wears an intricate collar and a kilt with pleats and long flowing sashes tied together behind his apron at his waist. His queen, Ankhesenamun, offers him a garland of flowers. She is wearing a wig embedded with jewellery, a collar and a sheer long robe.*

Wigs were worn by both men and women. Many were intricate arrangements of human hair strands and plaits, padded out and supported by inner layers of vegetable fibres such as date palm. Usually each wig had 300 strands, each amounting to 400 hairs. The hair strands were looped and waxed onto an inner net at such a high temperature that even the most severe Egyptian summer could not melt them out of place.

Often a woman's cropped hair was mounted with a long, thick wig. Egyptians believed it would increase her sexuality. Men's wigs were smaller, but their coiffure could be even more complex.

Festivals and banquets were the special occasions for wearing a wig. It was made more appealing by being scented with perfume. Wall paintings show high cones perched on the crown of each wig. However, it has recently been suggested by English Egyptologist Joann Fletcher that these were hieroglyphs signalling that each wig was perfumed.

▼ *Papyrus depicting Ani and his wife wearing their long, pleated robes as they play the game of senet. Both men and women wore long garments made from cool, light linen.*

➤ *Banquets — New Kingdom Parties* ◄

The Egyptian elite wore their elaborate wigs to banquets where they sat, drank and ate, dressed in their pleated finery. From New Kingdom wall paintings these banquets were a joyously frequent entertainment. Each guest at the dinner party was met by the hosts and showered with garlands by the hosts' servants. Their wigs were scented and they were brought into the dining room. There they sat on chairs, stools or cushions by small tables from which they were served wine and an assortment of meats, fruits, breads and vegetables piled like a buffet. Music accompanied their feasting. The guests' eyes were graced with elegantly slim girls, some almost naked, playing the lute, flute, harp or tambourine. Dancers swirled and acrobats leapt before them. Their senses were drenched with the colour, song, dance and perfumed sweetness of life. These were the scenes which so often decorated New Kingdom nobles' tomb walls. This was the life they wished to continue eternally in the afterlife.

◄ *Lute players were essential to an Egyptian party. This pottery vase has been shaped in the form of a female lute player.*

▼ *This wall painting of a banquet underway shows Egyptian ladies and gentlemen attended by servants offering them wine and flowers.*

➤ *Keeping Up Appearances* ◄

Egyptians used to wash at least once a day. Water was plentiful, but some sources, like canals or ponds, were alive with snails which left the larvae of tiny organisms' in their wake. These damaged the skin of those who washed or drank there. Most Egyptians would never see a bathroom in their lifetimes. Only the elite bathed in such luxurious surroundings attended by their servants. It was common practice, no matter what their social class, to wash the body and the mouth in the morning with a naturally occurring mixture known as natron. This contains sodium carbonate and bicarbonate among other substances.

Vegetable oils, or hippopotamus, crocodile or cat fat was used as rubbing lotions to stop skin dryness and to maintain skin suppleness and youth. Egyptian nobles were pictured

▶ *A naked girl carved from wood is swimming and holds aloft a cosmetic container, used perhaps for holding fragrant oils.*

▼ *A rare moment in Egyptian art: in this wall painting two female musicans playing at a banquet face the viewer directly with their alluring eyes. Perhaps it captured the wild abandon of their music when all the conventions of society were loosened, if only for an instant. We can even see the soles of their feet.*

◀ *Perfumes were stored in these beautiful glass containers introduced during the time of the New Kingdom.*

being massaged by their servants. Deodorants were also supplied, but there were no perfumes made from an alcohol base. Perfumes were derived from natural substances such as dates, myrrh or frankincense. Embalmed bodies were anointed with fragrant scents and herbs.

Women's eyelids were painted. In the New Kingdom *medemet*, now known in Egypt as *kohl*, was made from lead and antimony sulphides. Hatshepsut's expedition to Punt brought back much lead sulphide. It also served to disinfect the wearer, keep insects away, especially flies, and its characteristically Egyptian black line rimming the eye shielded it from the sun's glare.

▼ *A female lute player is shown kneeling on a cushion on this blue faience dish. She has a Bes figure tattooed on her naked thigh. A monkey reaches for her hip sash. Bes tattoos were erotic and common to some dancers and musicians.*

➤ *Skin, Tattoos and Eros* ◄

Mummified bodies, wall paintings, ostraca and dishes reveal that tattooing was practised mostly on musicians, dancers, singers and prostitutes. It had an erotic element, often punctured onto the thigh with the symbol of Bes' face. He was not only the dwarf god of childbirth, but was related to fertility and sexual love. Some "dolls", known as "brides of the dead" were also tattooed and placed in New Kingdom burials. Tattoos were also left on women's chins, noses, torsos, limbs and breasts. There is a model of a harpist with the magic eye of Horus tattooed over the centre of her chest. The skin itself was not pierced by pieces of jewellery until the New Kingdom. Mummies of this period have significant perforations made to hold rings, ear-rings and studs.

➤ *Jewellery* ◄

Female and male bodies were also adorned with exquisite jewellery. Early in Egyptian history beads were made from bones, sea shells and egg shells, and also manufactured copper, and faience which was made from pulverised quartz, a little lime and ash or natron, often with a shiny blue glaze.

▼ *Busy in their workshop, jewellers bore holes in beads with three or four bow-drills at a time. The beads were polished and strung to form the collars held by the jeweller (lower left). A metalworker blows through a pipe to increase the heat of his fire.*

◀ *A scene from
Egyptian heavy
industry: at a safe
distance using metal
rods, metalworkers hold
a crucible of molten ore
over a fire. Its fire is
raised by men treading
on foot-bellows.
Below them workmen
are in the process of
making bricks.*

Bracelets and anklets were carved from stone and bone. Bracelets and necklaces belonging to Egyptian nobles were fashioned in gold.

Once, only the king had the right to wear this precious metal. It was considered to be the flesh of the sun, immortal. It was mined in desolate areas east of the Nile, on the Red Sea shores and south in Nubia. There are many wall paintings of Nubians bearing gold to their Egyptian rulers. Gold could be liquefied under heat and then poured into a mould, or be skilfully beaten into shape, or have its precious grains soldered into place.

➤ *Magic Amulets* ◀

Much jewellery did have a religious purpose, related to the function of amulets. They magically shielded the wearer from the actual dangers of Egyptian life such as deadly snakes and scorpions, and also evil spirits which may enter the body at its weakest, unprotected parts.

Amulets were shaped in the form of Bes for childbirth and sexuality, and the Eye of Horus for healing, wholeness and well-being. They could be worn on the body's vital points or on a necklace with a few special amulets to protect and bring blessings on the wearer.

These necklaces were sometimes banded together in rows to become a broad collar. This collar could be quite heavy in front. A *mankhet* balanced the weight in the form of a pendant behind at the back.

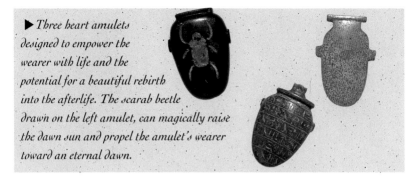

▶ *Three heart amulets designed to empower the wearer with life and the potential for a beautiful rebirth into the afterlife. The scarab beetle drawn on the left amulet, can magically raise the dawn sun and propel the amulet's wearer toward an eternal dawn.*

Pectorals, like Tutankhamun's beautiful right and left Eyes of Horus, were counterpoised by such a pendant dropping down the back along a cord slung around the neck.

⤞ *Pharaoh the Athlete* ⇇

Although supporting a large ornate pectoral must have been a strenuous activity for the king, there were other more robust, physical pursuits. The warrior pharaohs prided themselves on their physical strength and balance. Amenhotep II, Thutmose III's son, could masterfully draw back his composite bow and fire it from a racing chariot, steered from reins tied around the king's waist, shooting his arrows with pin point

▶ *Above the eyes of his queen, Tutankhamun demonstrates his athletic prowess, drawing back and aiming his powerful composite bow during a hunt. This detail is from a chest found in the tomb of Tutankhamun.*

accuracy. Arrow on arrow, in a straight file, pierced copper ingots as if they were leaves of papyrus, according to a proud Amenhotep II. His father, inaugurating this sporting tradition, had performed a similar feat.

Such physical exertion was typical of the restless, energetic Bronze Age when New Kingdom pharaohs not only fought and triumphed in battle, but ran the Heb Sed course like their ancestors, to prove, after a reign of thirty years, that they were still strong enough to claim the Throne of the Two Lands. They also hunted elephants in Syria, and even the teenager, Tutankhamun, pictured himself hunting wild beasts from his racing chariot.

➤ *The Sun Folk in Action* ◄

The king was not alone in demonstrating his athletic prowess and courage. Loyal Egyptians were like Amenemhab who followed his king into the dangerous field of the Syrian elephant hunt and, in battle before Kadesh, charged forward to disembowel a provocative Syrian mare.

New Kingdom Egyptians ran, jumped, wrestled, fought each other with sticks, boxed, swam and rowed. They also participated in ball games. Texts and pictures older than the New Kingdom attest to games played with balls, like the two girls at Beni Hasan, riding on their friends' bent backs and tossing balls to each other, while the Old Kingdom *Pyramid Texts* affirm that the dead enjoy ball games in the afterlife.

The best balls which have survived were covered with slices of leather, sewn around a stuffed centre of hair, yarn, straw, chaff or reeds. Later balls may have had seeds or beads inside, which rattled when they were thrown.

◄ *The New Kingdom noble, Nebamun, with three heron decoys in his right hand, is about to hurl his stick carved in the form of a snake into a flock of marsh birds. Nobles prided themselves on their physical prowess.*

▶ *New Kingdom Egyptians had a sense of humour. On this detail from a painted papyrus the artist pokes fun at the realm of the afterlife. An antelope and a lion play senet — a popular game which resembled the winding ways of the afterlife.*

The earliest picture of a bat and ball game has Thutmose III holding a ball in this left arm and a long bat of wavy olive wood in his right. The king is facing Hathor. Priests hold balls, apparently caught after the king has struck them.

≥ Senet — a Board Game ≼

Judging from the number of references to the game of Senet, it must have been the most popular board game in New Kingdom Egypt. It was to be enjoyed in a relaxed atmosphere while sipping wine and beer in the shade, sheltering from a hot day. *Senet* in Egyptian means "to pass" or "to go by or around". The aim of the game was for each player to zigzag his pieces past his opponents' pieces and a series of dangerous positions on a grid of 30 squares: 3 long rows of ten squares. The place of our dice was taken by throwing sticks or a bone from a sheep's foot, an astragal. It may have involved taking the opposing pieces and finally throwing the right number to proceed to the winning "31st" square outside the field of play.

Senet had a religious dimension. It was buried with the dead and appeared on tomb walls and in the *Book of the Dead*. It represented a conflict between good and evil forces. Some pieces had the heads of demons. If you landed on square 27, a field of water, you fell back to square 15, "House of Rebirth", where you started all over again for the winning "31st" square, the symbolic end of the journey, not only of the game, but also of one's inevitable mortal path past the perils of the underworld toward immortality in the presence of the great god Osiris.

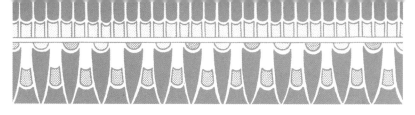

Temples, Festivals, Priests and Visions

➤ Truth in the Temple ◄
— the Goddess Maat and the King

Many Egyptian temples have scenes of Maat, the goddess of Truth and Order carved on their walls. She is praised as the daughter of Re. Since the King is the son of Re, she is often portrayed as the king's sister. She is pictured with the king, as Isis had accompanied Osiris.

➤ Hieroglyphs, Architecture and the Gods ◄
— Heaven on Earth

Maat's hieroglyphs sometimes picture her as a feather, the feather of Truth; or as a flat base platform, ending in a ramp — it supports a god's throne before it finally slants down to the floor, the cosmic symbol of balance and harmony. Even the base of an Egyptian temple

◄ *This pectoral depicts the goddess Maat standing before a throned Tutankhamun with her wings outstretched, moving the air, his life, toward him as ruler of the Two Lands. Maat is the personification of Truth and Order.*

floor mirrored this shape of truth. The floor rose slightly toward the inner sanctum along a series of ramps. The goddess Maat, it could be said, formed the very basis of the sacred structure.

This was the Egyptian way of recognising and understanding ideas like Truth. The Egyptian temple should be seen as a magnified hieroglyph of architectural order and harmony. The temple pylons were wide twin towers, intersected by a central gateway. Amon-Re's temple at Karnak had such a gateway facing west. To the Egyptian imagination this architectural construction resembled two round sloping mountain peaks through which the sun's disc set or rose — this shape forms the hieroglyph *akhet*, which means the horizon. The Karnak temple was a solar temple based on the principles of balance and harmony — it was the horizon of Amon-Re, his home on earth. To encourage this king of the gods to stay, the Egyptians built what they considered to be heaven on earth. Its pylons approached heaven. Its tall flagstaffs rose to be the peers of the stars themselves.

At the Interface Between Life and the Afterlife — the Temple as a "Horizon"

The sun on the horizon gave a brilliant hint of another realm beyond ordinary Egyptian life. The Egyptians saw it as a mystic opening, brightly slicing the skin of Creation. Here was a glimpse of the afterlife.

▼ *The long axis of the Karnak temple runs eastward between the First Pylon's tall towers back into the sacred depths of Amon-Re's inner precinct.*

◀ *Balance and harmony are set in stone at the solar god Horus' Edfu temple. The towers of the pylons represent mountains; the space between them above the gateway opens to the sky, place of the sun. Here the sky and the earth meet and the sun will rise between the pylon "mountains", like the hieroglyph,* akhet.

The dawn sun rose, released from the underworld of night. The sun set, sliding back into the deep dark underworld. This was the moment when heaven and earth met, when life on this earth briefly witnessed the aura of the afterlife through heaven's gate.

The Egyptian temple, as the "house" of its god, was the place where the god appeared on earth. It was seen as the horizon of the god. The god "dwelt" deep inside the temple structure, in the shape of a statue. Only the king or select priests could behold the divine image. Here human encountered the divine, the living met the eternal.

➤ Through to the Beginning of Creation ◀ — the Hypostyle Hall

Walking from the west, through the First Pylon at Karnak, the visitor is struck by the vast courtyard. Then moving further east, past the great open space through the second Pylon's gate, one would be overwhelmed by the next area — an enormous forest of geometrically packed thick columns. They numbered 134, sprouting papyrus plant capitals at the top of their stone stems. The cathedral Notre Dame de Paris would have almost fitted inside this hall alone. The scale of the place, known as the Hypostyle Hall, dwarfed and bewildered any visitor.

▲ *Looking north across Karnak's sacred lake, a forest of distant colossal columns marks the rise of the Hypostyle Hall (left) as two obelisks — Thutmose I's (centre) and Hatshepsut's (right) pierce the sky.*

However, an Egyptian priest would have known what this symbolised, walking along the East-West corridor. He would have pointed up to the ceiling nearly 25 metres (over 80 ft) above this axial path. There rose the hall's broadest columns with papyrus capitals which splayed out below the ceiling. Further away from this axis, in this densely columned space, under a mysterious light filtering through high stone grates known as clerestory windows, the columns' width decreases toward the hall's northern and southern rims.

The priest would have explained that he was entering a sacred space. The sun's rays, the Black Land's first light, travelling east to west, would beam onto these axial papyrus stems. They have naturally opened in this solar temple. This axis marked the first light of the world.

◀ *The high capitals of these giant columns widen as if they were splayed fronds of papyrus plants opening to the light of the sun, along the central axis of the Hypostyle Hall.*

▼ *Away from the wide capitals of the colossal central columns, other capitals (left) are closed, unlit by the light of the sun which streams in at a higher level through clerestory windows.*

The priest was now at the edge of the earliest swamp of reeds. Other hypostyle halls have insects carved on their columns to enhance this effect. Some floors are water-logged at flood time. He was approaching the primeval mound, the *benben* of creation, which was the first place of his god on earth, his or her home on earth, the divine horizon.

Warrior pharaohs, such as Thutmose III, appeared on the outer face of pylon walls to rid Egypt of its enemies. These outer walls symbolised a protective zone on the other side of the pylon, facing the external world. The king, hero of truth and order, *maat*, repelled the forces of chaos.

The threatening world outside was made safe. History itself could be shut outside, beyond the temple walls. Colossal statues of the pharaohs were also placed outside the pylons. The pharaoh had been magnified by his connection with his god. He protected his god's house on earth.

The densely columned forest also closed off the rest of the world. Another light suffused the wisps of incense smoke filling the temple interior. The clerestory windows filtered away the normal brilliance of an Egyptian day's sunlight. Our priest was in another world inhaling an aromatic atmosphere in a haunting light. He came closer to the place where time and space began.

➤ *Obelisks — Shafts to the Divine* ◄

At Karnak, past the Hypostyle Hall, pairs of obelisks, tall shafts of hewn granite, shot up to the sky along the axial route. A pyramidion topped each obelisk's tapered ascent. It was known as the *benbenet*, related to the "primeval mound", the *benben*. It was sheathed with electrum, an alloy of silver and gold.

▶ *Rising above its fallen partner, this is the only standing obelisk of Hatshepsut, the queen who became king. After her death her nephew Thutmose III built a roof around the shafts of her obelisks as well as walls about their bases to prevent any sight of her royal titles.*

When the sun's first and last rays shone on these brilliant surfaces the effect must have been blinding and spectacular, since the obelisks were aligned, one after the other, in pairs, along the East-West axis.

On the pyramidion's surface a relief was sculpted. The god Amon-Re blessed his son the pharaoh, just as the sun blessed the Two Lands. A vertical line of hieroglyphs descended each shaft face with the five great names of Pharaoh. The glory of his titles soared up to each startling solar pyramidion.

Heart of Karnak: Ipet-Sut — Heart of Ipet-Sut: *Holy of Holies*

Below these dazzling granite skyscrapers, our priest would venture into the darkening corridor, past the Hypostyle Hall. Coming into the heart of Amon-Re's temple, "the most esteemed of places", *Ipet-Sut*, he would notice the floor level's slow rise along a series of gently ascending ramps, which are Maat's hieroglyphs. The ceiling, decorated with stars, steadily comes closer to the floor. The priest would be approaching the place where time and space began, the "primeval mound", at the heart of *Ipet-Sut*, the Holy of Holies, Amon-Re's boat shrine.

Ipet-Sut's halls and shrines were decorated with precious stones such as lapis lazuli, gold and electrum — the spoils of the early New Kingdom pharaohs' conquests. These gifts were lavished on the god who gave Egypt's kings victory.

◀ *The sacred statue of Amon-Re with his crown of feathers rising from a sun disc. Made of silver and gold it may have been placed inside one of his portable boat shrines.*

The lotus and the papyrus, heraldic flowers of Upper and Lower Egypt, their stems and blossoms rising up their separate square pillars, marked the entrance to the Holy of Holies, south and north of the axial way. To the west of these flowering pillars a room opened up, walled behind the Sixth Pylon. Descriptions of the campaigns of Thutmose III, in particular the Battle of Megiddo, were carved on these walls. This is the "Hall of the Annals" of Thutmose III. Nearby a black granite stele proclaimed how Amon-Re crushed the enemies of Egypt for his son, his champion, Thutmose III. The walls of the Annals' Hall echoed with the power and might of the god who lived beyond, above the stairs, ascending between the square pillars, in the Holy of Holies where Thutmose III was crowned and consecrated.

Very few priests, let alone the ordinary people, saw this revered place, the horizon of the god, Amon-Re. His gold statue was hidden inside a small kiosk inside a sun boat. This consecrated vessel rested in the darkest, most sacred shrine of the Karnak complex. It left its horizon on special festive occasions.

▶ *These square pillars at the entrance of the Holy-of-Holies (Amon-Re's boat shrine at Katnak) represent the lotus and the papyrus — symbols of Upper and Lower Egypt.*

➤ *Holidays, Holy Days — Egyptian Festivals* ➤

It was believed that the gods travelled over the sky and through the underworld in boats. On special days, the image inside its boat shrine and, in particular, at Karnak, made its way, held aloft by a gang of priests on an elaborately decorated boat, along a processional path, from the temple's dark recesses to the sunlit world of ordinary Egyptians.

The routine of the Egyptian ten day week after week was relieved by a generous schedule of festival days, holidays. These celebrated a god, a new year, the start of a new season, the Nile, a coronation or a royal anniversary, or a city. They gave the ordinary people a chance to enjoy, and perhaps even transform, their lives. They feasted on grapes, watermelons, figs, pomegranates, as well as rarities to their diets such as meats. These were times of joy, spectacle, prayers and pleas to the god, reverie and, now and then, a miracle.

▼ *The processional avenues linking the important sacred sites of Amon in Thebes were lined with vigilant and colossal statues of ram-headed sphinxes, sacred to Amon-Re. These sphinxes witnessed the festive parades when Amon-Re's statue was carried in his boat shrine outside the temple for all to see and worship.*

➤ *"Amon, the God Who Hears"* ⬅
— *Ordinary People at Prayer*

Ordinary Egyptians, not part of the exclusive temple priesthoods, were not allowed into most areas of the temple precinct. However, we have evidence on the exterior walls of New Kingdom temples where sculpted ears have been found. Surrounding these "shrines" are prayers to the god "who hears". The ancient Egyptians believed that these ears were their point of access to the god living in his house, his temple.

➤ *The Opet Festival* ⬅
— *Amon-Re Visits His Southern Harem at Luxor*

Opet was the most important festival on the Egyptian calendar. Late in the New Kingdom (*c*.1570–1070 BC), it lasted twenty seven days and involved giving out 11 341 bread loaves, 85 cakes and 385 beer jugs. It centred around a journey of Amon-Re, his wife Mut, and their son Khons, from Karnak to Luxor, three kilometres (2 miles) south. This holy family of Thebes left Karnak, their statues concealed in their individual shrines. The priests carried them through the temple and then they were placed in their own boats on the river journey south. On the water these sacred ships were towed by smaller boats, and on the river bank by human hands and muscles, including those of the king's officials. Their progress on the water was accompanied by singing and dancing, and by squads of soldiers. It was a time when ordinary Egyptians beg the gods and the king for favours in this highly charged festive atmosphere. The Nile's flood waters had miraculously swollen and there was no work to do in the fields. The people could sail over the land. Hope was in the air. Amon was visiting his southern harem. The king, usually away at his northern capital, Memphis, was travelling with his god south.

On the Luxor temple walls, one king, Amenhotep III (*c*.1387–1350 BC), great grandson of Thutmose III, reminded everyone that his body and *ka* were fathered by Amon-Re. The god had impregnated his mother. Inside the temple the king's *ka* was magically brought into being by Amon-Re. This royal *ka* was more than just a life force, as it was for an ordinary person. This *ka* had a supernatural force only shared

by the gods. Here, under the spell of incense, ritual, belief and temple architecture the king was fused fully with the spirit of his own divinity, his royal *ka*, created by Amon-Re. The king re-emerged from the temple's depths renewed for another year by his mystic union with the King of Gods, Amon-Re. And the people rejoiced. They feasted. They prayed that their pleas would be answered on these special days when the land and its lord were transformed.

⤛ The Beautiful Festival of the Valley ⤜ — Amon-Re Visits the West

Before harvest time the statue of Amon-Re was again taken from his "primeval mound" at Karnak's heart. His progress was along the East-West axis of the temple. He continued in this solar direction across the Nile with his consort and child. On the west bank, they approached along an avenue or a canal, in an almost straight line from the Holy of Holies, the terraced mortuary temples of the founder of the Middle

▼ *Later in Egyptian history some priests grew powerful. On this stone relief the high priest of Amon-Re, Amenhotep, is installed in his office before the king, Rameses IX. The priest, now face to face with the king, is on near equal terms with his lord.*

Kingdom, Mentuhotep I (*c*.2060–2010 BC), and Thutmose III's aunt, Queen Hatshepsut (*c*.1498–1483 BC). These structures were skilfully positioned to set off the soaring curtain of cliffs to dramatic effect around the bay of Deir el Bahri. Behind these heights the New Kingdom pharaohs were buried in the Valley of the Kings. As time went on, later New Kingdom pharaohs' mortuary temples were visited by this holy family of Thebes.

This festival was shorter than Opet. It lasted ten days. Pharaoh, wearing his *atef* crown of feathers, uraeus, sun disc, ram and cattle horns, asked Amon-Re to visit these royal complexes on the west bank, including his own mortuary temple. There the god stayed overnight, receiving visits from the gods of the dead. This assembly gathered to perform rites for the multitudes interred in their tombs.

Many ordinary Egyptians, encouraged by Amon-Re's presence, visited their recently deceased relatives' and ancestors' tombs in the west. They shared a family dinner in the tomb's courtyard and slept the night there.

➤ *Priests — "Servants of the God"* ◄

Pharaoh as chief priest of every Egyptian god could not be present at each Egyptian god's temple to perform his duties. Priests took his place. They were not necessarily learned in the sacred texts and theological subtleties, but they performed the myriad of routine temple functions. Each was simply known as a "servant of the god", *hem netjer*.

Some performed the special daily rituals of awakening the god at dawn, of bathing, dressing and feeding the holy image of the god, and putting it to rest during the night. However, most priests never saw the divine statue. Their duties were occupied with the practical running of the temple.

It must be remembered that the temple, because of the vast wealth that was poured into it in the wake of the pharaohs' foreign victories and its own agricultural and industrial resources, had a vital economic place in Egypt. The temple employed many workers in its further construction projects, in its fields, workshops and mines. It had large granaries and butcheries which were especially active during festival times.

A priest wore clean finely woven clothes, cut to an old-fashioned style. Every part of his body was shaven. He had to have been circumcised and abstain from foods forbidden by the temple god, including meat from the animal whose form the god often took, such as Amon-Re the ram or Horus the falcon. He could not have sexual intercourse inside the temple nor was he allowed in the temple after sexual intercourse unless he washed. Water was important in keeping the priest ritually pure. Temples had a sacred lake for this purpose.

Priests also had a clear code of ethics. They were not to gossip about their sacred tasks in the temple, not to favour Egypt's great and powerful over ordinary people, not to take bribes, not to aim at making a profit, and not to turn the weighing scales in their favour.

Egypt's priesthood was a significant force in New Kingdom society, especially the priests of Amon-Re. Their god brought victory to each warrior pharaoh, who was chief priest of Amon-Re. Naturally the priesthood guarded its own privileges. Priests had a clean, healthy lifestyle.

▼ *East of the Hypostyle Hall, Thutmose III built his Festival Hall. It was patterned on the earliest form of Egyptian temple and oriented, as part of Amon-Re's solar temple, to the place of winter solstice sunrise.*

They lived in some of the most beautiful structures in Egypt, where they were fed and secure, both physically and spiritually. As men who married and fathered children, they jealously restricted the entry of outsiders into their exclusive priesthood. They kept its offices within their own families. Some formed priestly dynasties which extended seventeen generations across Egyptian history.

"Festival Hall" — Towards the End of Longest Night

Thutmose III's "Festival Hall" was devoted to the richness of life. It contained rooms whose walls were decorated with scenes from his distant conquests, the world subdued by Egypt as far as "the sun encircles". It celebrated the strangeness of empire, the animals and plants of exotic Asia, surveyed by the travelling Amon-Re.

East of *Ipet-Sut*, the Festival Hall was also concerned with beginnings. It has been suggested that Thutmose III had it aligned to the south-east towards winter solstice sunrise, the furthest, weakest southern rising on Karnak's eastern horizon. Its columns and ceiling resembled the poles and covering of a primitive Egyptian temple, a tent shrine. Its walls reveal royal ancestors. The structure, its shape and decoration, reaches back into the origins of Egyptian religion and kingship.

It is oriented with an awareness of the depths of time, king after dead king, in this "first temple", gazing back into the longest night waiting for the sun. This may explain why the primeval form of the sun, Sokar, a god from the depths of the underworld, is also present on the walls. Outside, twin figures of the king, sculpted as Osiris, Lord of the Underworld, stand either side of the Hall's entrance.

In his own tomb in the Valley of the Kings, Thutmose III had the twelve hours of the sun's journey through the underworld, the *Book of What is in the Netherworld*, the *Am Duat*, painted on the walls of his deep burial chamber. In the night's fifth hour the sun in the underworld passes over a dangerous depth in "the land of Sokar". Here the travelling sun emerged from the mound of night. Cold death has been defeated.

▲ *Inside a burial chamber cut out of solid rock in an elongated oval shape like a royal cartouche, or like the shape of the underworld itself, Thutmose III's sarcophagus sits surrounded by the twelve divisions of the* Book of What is in the Netherworld. *Each division represented one hour of night. Here the king magically travelled around the underworld under a starry ceiling for eternity.*

So Thutmose III had his architects focus on the horizon where the sun rises after its longest, darkest night, on the day when it casts its longest shadow at noon, the winter solstice. The Egyptian cosmos had gone through its darkest hours. The days would now get longer. The universe's life force had been resurrected. There was hope for humankind, living and dead. This hope has lit Karnak's Festival Hall. It will reach its climax at the other end of the year.

➤ *Sunrise to Sunset — the Axis of Creation* ◄

The shape of Karnak's Pylons were structured by the New Kingdom architects to resemble the hieroglyph "horizon", *akhet*. Karnak faced a naturally-formed *akhet*, the rolling mountains of Western Thebes, the Western Horizon. A wide open space rolled down between the sloping shoulders of their cliffs. Here the sun set. Earth and sky touched above

the processional path of the Beautiful Festival of the Valley in the blazing sunsets before the flood arrived, during the year's longest days.

A dazzling fissure, the sunset, burnt through the substance of creation. Heaven's gate opened. The light of the underworld, the afterlife, eternity, flashed back through this otherworldly opening, along the processional path. It lit every obelisk's electrum pyramidion. It fired through the Hypostyle Hall. There the elevated largest stone papyrus capitals, built for the occasion, splayed open. Here, the architecture came to life. The capitals, as papyrus, rose along the axis radiantly, blooming in the brilliant path of the sun. Then the sunlight flared into *Ipet-Sut*, the temple's inner sanctum. Concentrated into a sharpening beam, by the constricting levels of floor and ceiling, it slanted toward and ignited the "primeval mound", the Holy of Holies.

▼ *At the twelfth division of the* Book of What is in the Netherworld, *the "flesh of the sun" in the form of a ram-headed human magically leaves his solar boat and travels along the coils of a massive snake toward the eastern horizon. He is transformed into the Sun-Disc pushed by the scarab beetle to pierce the underworld's oval rim and become the risen sun at dawn. After the longest night this sun would blaze trimphantly down the Festival Hall's corridors and chambers.*

The heart of *Ipet-Sut* was returned to the first brilliant momentary rays of sunlight which shaped life on earth, on this first horizon of time and space, the *benben*. The solar boat was charged with the force of the "first time". It glowed, reflecting back the first light of creation, from east to west, into the slipping light of the setting sun, as the light of eternity was sinking over the Deir el Bahri cliffs, veiling the Valley of the Kings, its eternal destination, the royal tombs.

In his solar boat Amon-Re could now revisit the west along the path of this eternal light. Here was a cosmic rehearsal of Amon-Re's earth-bound Beautiful Festival of the Valley. Now the sun in its sacred boat could enter eternity. Heaven's door was still open.

The sun, now charged with the Holy of Holies' first light, and lit by eternity, could magically assume its underworld afterlife form, borne aloft on its boat, to voyage across the dark hours of night. It could bless and illuminate those living deep in the eternal netherworld, as mystically imagined in Thutmose III's *Am Duat*, after horizon had lit horizon, west to east, east to west, first light out of eternal light, along the axial path of Karnak and the west bank, from winter sunrise to summer sunset, the axis of creation.

◀ *The sky goddess Nut swallows the sun at sunset. The sun floats through her long celestial body to be reborn between her thighs at dawn. She is the divine embodiment of the unbroken axis of creation — sunrise to sunset to sunrise.*

From Queen to King — Daughter of Re: Hatshepsut

➤ *The Silence of the Record — a King Disappears* ◄

Under later pharaohs any list of Eighteenth Dynasty (*c*.1570–1294 BC) rulers records the simple succession of Thutmose I, Thutmose II and Thutmose III. However, this official version of Egyptian history omits one of the Two Lands' most intriguing pharaohs — the daughter of Thutmose I, half-sister and wife of Thutmose II, and stepmother and aunt of Thutmose III — Hatshepsut (*c*.1498–1483 BC), "Foremost of Leading Noblewomen".

Her statues were smashed. Her name and sculpted wall reliefs were erased with chisels. Some of her chapels were dismantled. Even her obelisks at

▶*Hatshepsut's divine eyes gaze confidently from her sculpted head, which was once part of a colossal statue. It came from the terraces of her mortuary temple at Deir el-Bahri. Here it formed part of the dramatic stage where her royal power merged with Amon-Re's divinity.*

Karnak were boarded up and a temple ceiling fixed around them to cut off a close view of her royal titles climbing the granite shafts towards electrum-plated heights. This was where Amon-Re, her god and divine father, consecrated her as a slim, bare-chested warrior pharaoh.

➤ *Daughter to a New Age — Thutmose I's Egypt* ◄

As a young Egyptian princess Hatshepsut must have looked with pride on the achievements of her father. Thutmose I's reign marked a new beginning for Egypt. In pursuit of the Hyksos and their allies he had seen new worlds, the "inverted" flow of the Euphrates and the upper reaches of the Nile. He had asserted Egyptian power further north and south than any other king. Back home he had started an important building program, especially at Karnak. Here his obelisks soared and his walls encompassed new sacred spaces for Amon-Re.

At Tombos near the Nile's Third Cataract, he erected a stele on which he claimed not only to have ventured to the world's ends but to have entered the underworld. Very early fragments of his burial chamber's *Am Duat (Book of What is in the Netherworld)* have been discovered. As he mapped out new landscapes on the earth's surface this stele's reference to the underworld could point to one of the great spiritual achievements of the New Kingdom (*c.*1570–1070 BC) — opening up new realms beyond life, charting new courses in the underworld. Bricks stamped with his name have been found at the new workers' village of Deir el Medina. The task of these craftsmen was to excavate the royal rock cut tombs in the Valley of the Kings.

As an important member of a new royal family, apparently unrelated to Amenhotep I (Thutmose I's predecessor), Hatshepsut would have been anxious that her family succeed in setting this new destiny for Egypt. She must have been honoured to have been associated with her father. Later she had herself pictured sitting majestically before his throne.

◄ *Hatshepsut with the blue war crown and athletic physique of a warrior pharoah kneels before her father, Amon-Re. His lifted arms form the hieroglyph* ka *or life force over her — "his son", "his daughter".*

◀ *This axe blade, decorated with the familiar pose of Pharaoh ritually smiting his enemy, has the royal names of Ahmose, founder of the New Kingdom inscribed inside two cartouches. It was found in Queen Ahhotep I's tomb reflecting the militant eternity of an Egyptian Queen, one of a line of strong, royal women.*

⋙ *Royal Wife of Thutmose II* ⋘ *— Hatshepsut, Queen of Egypt*

Hatshepsut's parents, Thutmose I (*c*.1525–1519 BC) and Queen Ahmose had no son. However, her father had a son with a minor wife, Mutnofret. He became the next king, Thutmose II (*c*.1519–1505 BC). As was the custom in Egyptian royal families, Hatshepsut married her half-brother. They had a daughter, Neferure. Thutmose II and a minor wife, Isis, had a son. Because Thutmose II died young, this son became Thutmose III when he ascended the throne at the age of nine in about 1505 BC.

⋙ *A Line of Strong Women — Egypt's Queens* ⋘

Hatshepsut, as the aunt and stepmother of Thutmose III, became regent to the young king, governing the Two Lands in his name. She had thus joined a great tradition of women who played a major role in the fight against the Hyksos, bringing order and stability to the Two Lands, setting Egypt on its imperial trajectory.

Tetisheri, King Ahmose's grandmother, had been his regent in his early years as king, as Egypt prepared for the final strike to oust the Hyksos. She had, no doubt, witnessed the hastily mummified body of her own son, King Seqenenre (*c*.1575 BC), fatally wounded on the battlefield, being borne to his grave.

When Tetisheri died her daughter, Queen Ahhotep II, mother of King Ahmose, took over the regency. There is evidence that she quelled a rebellion in Upper Egypt during the anti-Hyksos wars. Another queen, Ahhotep I, had jewellery and weapons — daggers and battle axes — as well as Golden Flies, the rewards for bravery, buried with her.

▲ *Beside the portable boat shrine a harpist plays, acrobats leap and women with raised sistrums sing to the haunting tinkle of a chorus of shaking metallic sistrums. Priests will carry the boat shrine on their shoulders out of the temple under the eyes of the co-regents, Hatshepsut and Thutmose III, on one of Amon-Re's festival days.*

From Regent to Co-regent — Hatshepsut Becomes King

The memory of these capable queens persisted, honoured by their descendants, well into Hatshepsut's time. However, during the regency she went one step further. She had proclaimed herself king, at least by the seventh year of Thutmose III's reign. Thutmose III was not pushed aside. They reigned together in a co-regency.

Co-regencies had been introduced after the fall of the Old Kingdom (c.2125 BC) during the Middle Kingdom to secure the line of succession more firmly from pharaoh to pharaoh. They appeared together in wall reliefs, often physically identical, only their royal names in cartouches distinguishing them from each other. Hatshepsut usually played the dominant role.

➤ *Beyond the Silence of the Record* ◄ — *Hatshepsut's Motives*

It is difficult to penetrate the veneer of the official statements on Hatshepsut's later monuments to identify her motives for assuming the kingship. Some historians have denounced her as a scheming usurper, an evil stepmother driven by a ruthless will to power. This reveals more about these historians' own times and prejudices than about Hatshepsut and her world.

Egypt had previously been ruled by female kings. Yet the Two Lands was not on the verge of chaos. Hatshepsut was not there on the throne as the last hope of an ailing dynasty. Nor could she claim a special position as the ultimate royal "heiress" with the most royal blood to claim the throne, because the mothers of Thutmose II and Thutmose III were lesser royal wives. English Egyptologist Gay Robins has argued that there was no such succession of "heiress" queens. Hatshepsut's parents were not directly related to the previous rulers themselves.

Her family was a new start for Egypt. Her strong personality, family loyalty, the positions she held — Regent and God's Wife of Amon — as well as her advisers who depended on her position and power, may all have propelled her toward becoming king. The Throne of the Two Lands may have, as a result, been more securely founded within the Tuthmoside family than ever.

Hatshepsut may have understood that she was maintaining and furthering the traditions established by her father, Thutmose I. She too had ordered Egyptians to a remote rim of the world, built chapels, erected obelisks, praised Amon-Re and perhaps even led the army on campaign. She had been the daughter, the half-sister, the wife, the aunt, the stepmother to three Thumoside kings. She held the recently introduced title, "God's Wife of Amon".

➤ *"God's Wife of Amon"* —*Amon Re and the Queen* ◄

As Regent Hatshepsut preferred using this title, first introduced with Amenhotep I's mother, Ahmose Nefertari, in phrases which usually referred to a living pharaoh. She was also given property and

administrators to look after it. This title also allowed Hatshepsut to enter into the presence of the god, a rare privilege, and it links Hatshepsut and her family with the earlier New Kingdom royal family of Ahmose.

It was a priestly office which may have had sexual implications. Hatshepsut was the "God's Wife". Another of her titles, "the God's Hand" may have involved her, as Robins suggests, in stimulating her god. Atum's hand, personified as a goddess, brought forth life's earliest forces, air and moisture, on earth. There is a hint of this sexual relationship in the very name Hatshepsut. It is a shortened form of *Hatshepsut Khenemet-Amun*, "joined with Amon, Foremost of Noble-women". There is a relief of Hatshepsut reaching toward ithyphallic Amon-Re.

This new intimacy with the god is reflected in the introduction of a new form of the Egyptian language used during Hatshepsut's time. The official language of early New Kingdom monuments was Middle Egyptian, a form of the Egyptian language which reached its classic expression in the great literary works of the Middle Kingdom. However, New Kingdom Egyptians spoke in a tongue known as Late Egyptian. In her monuments Hatshepsut was one of its earliest users. There was then a new language, expressed if only fleetingly to reveal her direct, intimate access to Amon-Re.

▼ *Another red granite block shows Hatshepsut running to prove the strength of her vigour in the presence of a bull (right). These stones from the Red Chapel were once part of Amon-Re's inner sanctum, but were later dismantled to become the fill of later structures at the Karnak temple. Amon Re's solar boat sits on the left.*

➤ *Hatshepsut's Divine Birth* ◀

The new office, "God's Wife of Amon", which gave Hatshepsut new authority and power and a new relationship with Amon-Re, may also have encouraged Hatshepsut to rise to the Egyptian throne. In her mortuary temple dedicated to Amon-Re, *Djeser Djeseru*, Amon-Holy-of-Holies, which directly faces Amon-Re's temple at Karnak, there are a series of reliefs where she explored new meanings and dimensions of kingship in the framework of ancient stories and institutions.

One of these stories was her divine birth. In the Old Kingdom there was a myth that the generation of kings after Khufu and Khafre were born as triplets to a priestess of Re, fathered by the Sun God Re himself. Hatshepsut gave this myth a New Kingdom structure. She claimed her mother, Ahmose, who did not hold the priestly title, "God's Wife of Amun", was visited in her bed chamber by a fragrant Amon-Re. The god had chosen the body of her father. Thutmose I's throne name, *Aakheperkare*, "Great is the Becoming of the *ka* of Re", in fact fulfils the

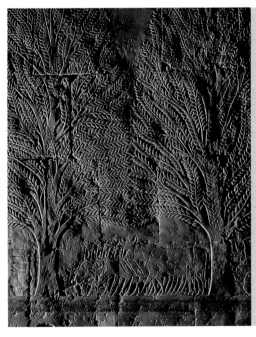

◀ *Hatshepsut's artists had sharp, dramatic eyes and hands as they sculpted the wall reliefs inside the colonnades at Deir el Bahri. Here cattle graze under vivid trees. Cattle were not only essential to the economy but to politics and religion. Many New Kingdom pharaohs were known as "Mighty Bull", while Hathor, Hatshepsut's favoured goddess of love and fertility, appeared as an important presence at Deir El Bahri, as a cow or a beautiful woman with cow ears.*

▲ *The wife of the Chief of Punt may have suffered from elephantiasis. This did not stop the sly humour of Hatshepsut's artists from placing her near her frail husband or her skinny donkey. Hatshepsut sent an expedition to Punt (thought to be Somalia) in the ninth year of her reign.*

purpose of Amon-Re. Thutmose I's physical appearance is a fitting human vessel to shape Amon-Re's potent divine form on earth.

And Amon-Re loved and impregnated Ahmose, making her his "wife". Hatshepsut was conceived as a result of this Sacred Marriage. Her physical body *khet* and her *ka* were formed on the potter's wheel by the ram-headed creator god, Khnum. Two young male figures, her *khet* and *ka*, were sculpted from the god's clay. Her royal *ka* was masculine. Khnum returned Hatshepsut and her *ka* to Queen Ahmose. He and his frog-headed wife, Heker, the goddess of fertility, led Ahmose to the place of her confinement. Here Hatshepsut was born, acclaimed by the gods as King of Upper and Lower Egypt, the Living Horus: Mighty of *Ka*'s.

Her claims to the throne were furthered in the colonnade at Deir el Bahri. She had herself pictured before her throned father. He announced to his court that she would be king. Hatshepsut had impelled herself into an imagined co-regency with her father.

☞ *The Expedition to Punt, the God's Command* ☜

Like her father, Hatshepsut's army ventured to the limits of the world. Ordered by an oracle of Amon, in the ninth year of her reign, she had sent an expedition, by land and sea, under the command of Neshy, to Punt, "the God's Land" — perhaps present day Somalia. There, among the natives' beehive huts raised on stilts, her men found myrrh destined to become incense for Amon-Re. Her troops, as pictured at Deir el Bahri, carry loose myrrh leaves and whole incense bearing trees, their roots wound into balls, bound in baskets and shouldered along into Egyptian ships. These myrrh trees were later planted in rows to form a garden fronting the rising terraces of Hatshepsut's Deir El Bahri mortuary temple complex, Amon-Holy-of-Holies.

☞ *Hatshepsut the Warrior* ☜

There is also evidence, Canadian Egyptologist Donald Redford argues, that Hatshepsut may have actually led an army south into Nubia. Two soldiers, Tiy and Djehuty, witnessed her defeating foreigners and collecting booty. Other inscriptions refer to military expeditions into Sinai, Palestine and Syria. One source claims that Hatshepsut's "arrow is among the Northern ones".

Thutmose III appears to have waged military campaigns later in their co-regency. He had ventured into Nubia and took Gaza in the north. Hatshepsut's reign was not simply a time of peace, as implied by the Punt expedition and her extensive building program, it involved operations typical of a warrior pharaoh. Hatshepsut had the right to wear the blue war crown.

◀ *Despite the overwhelming masculinity of many of her statues, there are also hints of a subtle feminine grace. On this face of one of her sphinxes Hatshepsut exudes a soft, yet alert feline power.*

➤ *Hatshepsut's Statues — from Queen to King* ◄

Her statues marked this transformation to a warrior pharaoh. She had her sculptors modify her feminine features. An early statue presents her as a queen: she wears a queen's headdress, the *khat*; she has small shoulders; her knees are covered, her hands laid flat out upon her knees; her breasts are obvious, and her Thutmoside face is small and soft-featured.

Tefnin, a Brussels-based Egyptologist, has traced the gradual change in her statues' appearance. There is a transitional phase where the sides of her *nemes* headdress are not as wide as a typical king's. Another statue appears quite male when viewed from the front. Here she presents broad shoulders, a flat, wide chest, thick arms and legs. Seen from the back, however, she has a graceful feminine figure.

Later statues portray her as a male Horus with the thick stump of a beard widening at its base over her chest. She is also sculpted as Osiris and a sphinx.

Later, as her reign continued, the symbol for the unity of Upper and Lower Egypt at the base of her throne, the interweaving lotus and papyrus stems, increased in size. Hatshepsut was growing more confident in proclaiming her ascension to the throne of Horus.

▶ *One of the many statues of Hatshepsut revealing her masculine features.*

➤ *Hatshepsut's Mortuary Temple* ◄ — *Amon-Holy-of-Holies*

Most of Hatshepsut's statues were found in the vicinity of her mortuary temple. Here, while she lived, Hatshepsut would unite with Amon-Re, King of Gods, during her visits to the temple. In death she joined Amon-Re here in Amon-Holy-of-Holies. It was built into the spectacular cliff face at Deir el Bahri, directly opposite the temple of her divine father, Amon-Re, at Karnak.

Hatshepsut also linked herself to the greatness of Egyptian history — to Mentuhotep I (*c.*2060–2010 BC), founder of the Middle Kingdom after the chaos in the wake of the collapse of the Pyramid Age — when she built her temple right alongside Mentuhotep I's temple. Transforming his design, the descending platforms of her wide courtyards advanced east toward Karnak.

Thutmose III built a temple, *Akhet Djeser*, Amon-Holy-Horizon, beside his co-regent's, Hatshepsut. These sacred sites were oriented toward the winter solstice sunrise, the place of the dawn's greatest triumph, where the sun returned from its longest night.

➤ *Maatkare as Architecture* ◄ — *Hatshepsut's Name Shapes a Temple*

The very structure and orientation of Hatshepsut's mortuary temple would have proclaimed to the Egyptian imagination the royalty of Hatshepsut. Seen from above her long rectangular courtyards form a frame resembling the hieroglyph, *ka*, the lifeforce — two extended parallel human arms and hands — assumed the three sides of a square or rectangle. Hatshepsut's Horus name was *Wesert Kau*, Mighty of *Ka*'s. The hieroglyph *ka*, on her Karnak obelisk, takes this rectangular shape. The *ka* hieroglyph is repeated three times in her Horus name. Could this echo the layout of her three courtyards at Deir el Bahri? *Ka* also occurs once in her throne name, Lord of the Two Lands. She is *Maatkare*: the *ka* of the *maat* of Re, the life force of Re's Truth, Order and Balance. Deir el Bahri's ramp resembles the bevelled hieroglyph for

▲ *The cliffs around Deir el Bahri could have easily dominated her structure, yet the brilliant ascent of colonnade on colonnade on three rising levels set off the high precipices behind it as a striking backdrop to a supernatural drama. It is as if the cliffs formed a massive stone curtain, raised to reveal Hatshepsut's wonder, Djeser Djeseru, "Holy-of-Holies", oriented toward Karnak and winter solstice sunrise.*

maat. The temple's orientation toward winter solstice sunrise, as well as its association with Amon Re, furthers this connection between Re, *maat* and *ka*. Now Hatshepsut projects herself as Lord of the Two Lands, *Maatkare*, in the form of this building. The red cliffs' ridges surround and embrace her structure like the *ka*'s long extending arms presenting the beauty of her Amon-Holy-of-Holies.

⤞ *Hatshepsut's* Ka — *the Lifeforce of Her Kingship* ⤝

Her emphasis on her *ka* reveals how Hatshepsut was able to legitimately claim to be king and to have herself sculpted as a male. Every Egyptian had a *ka*, a life force which animated the body and would survive death. The king had a royal *ka*, a more powerful lifeforce which he shared with his royal ancestors and the gods themselves. The royal *ka* was brought into being at conception. As Hatshepsut, and later Amenhotep III, had pictured, the *ka* was a being that existed alongside the physical body, *khet*, in a parallel world. It was shaped by Khnum on his potter's wheel and was masculine.

Hatshepsut could rightly present herself as king, the only female Horus, Mighty of *Ka's*. This may explain firstly, why she referred to herself in both masculine and feminine genders — Lord of the Two Lands, *Maatkare*; Daughter of Re, Hatshepsut. Secondly, why her statues emerged as masculine, for the *ka* could reside within a statue and her *ka* was male. She was in communication with forces beyond the normal gender divide of humankind. She could be a woman and a king simultaneously. Her claim was not a cynical fabrication. It was essential to New Kingdom ideas and beliefs about the subtle nature of royalty and power.

⤞ *Hatshepsut and the Goddess Hathor* ⤝

Her mortuary temple formed the stage for her many expressions of kingship: her divine conception and birth, her coronation, her expedition to Punt, the transport of her obelisks to Karnak and her relationship with the gods. There is a chapel at Deir el Bahri devoted to

> ▶ *Hathor, goddess of love and fertility, presided over Deir El Bahri. Hatshepsut took part of Deir El Bahri as the site of her temple, and here sculpted her image on the capitals of her Hathor shrine. Having assumed the divine animal power of Hathor, Hatshepsut serenely gazes on high, her cow ears protruding on her headdress, making her a superhuman being, a goddess herself. Hatshepsut has associated herself with both masculine and feminine divine powers.*

Hatshepsut and Hathor, the cow goddess, goddess of love, and goddess of the Western Mountain of the Western Theban area around Deir el Bahri. In this context, Hathor was believed to welcome, accept and look after the setting sun each evening.

Hatshepsut had herself portrayed on the back wall of the Hathor chapel between the solar deities, Amon-Re and Hathor. Hatshepsut's relationship intensified with Hathor in the high capitals on top of the columns in Hathor's shrine. Here Hatshepsut appeared as Hathor.

▼ *These four slim identical figures are of Neferure, known as the "God's Wife of Amon", after her mother. She would have been able to appear before Amon-Re in his Holy of Holies as well as her mother, the king.*

⋗ *Neferure the Princess* ⋖

Neferure was the only child of Thutmose II and Hatshepsut. We have much evidence of her existence from statues of her in relief and in the round. Six of these statues show her sporting a long lock of hair from the side of an otherwise bald head, known as the side lock of youth, and held by her nurse, Senenmut.

Her destiny may have been beyond what an Egyptian princess could expect. She was made "God's Wife of Amon" once her mother had relinquished this role and proceeded to the Throne of the Two Lands. Perhaps the child was intended to succeed her mother as another female Horus. For this reason it is doubtful whether Thutmose III married Neferure, his half-sister. Hatshepsut would have prevented this. It could bolster his claim to absolute sole rule against the claims of Neferure, daughter of Thutmose II, granddaughter of Thutmose I. Sadly the princess died young, and with her went any chance of Hatshepsut's own immediate family succeeding to the Double Crown.

⋗ *Senenmut the Favourite* ⋖

Senenmut, the nurse of Neferure, began his career with either Thutmose I or Thutmose II. He was born outside the royal circle and Thebes. He gained the royal family's confidence and became Neferure's nurse.

This position opened the way up to the high office of the Chief Steward of Amon. He organised the quarrying and transportation to Karnak of Hatshepsut's two massive obelisks. He may have played a part in the construction of her Deir el Bahri temple.

Many historians have connected Senenmut's rise with the widow Hatshepsut's ascent to the throne. The royal court has been dramatised with their muttering intrigues. It is intimated that they must have been lovers. The only evidence for this is an obscene sketch on an incomplete rock-cut tomb's wall.

However, this is to misunderstand the nature of the court of a Bronze Age pharaoh. It was natural and expected that favourites would be promoted. The ruler was exercising a hero's right to choose one subject

◀ *Senenmut, favoured nurse of Neferure, Hatshepsut's daughter, has been portrayed in this block statue in a pose protective of his royal charge, Neferure. The girl wears the side lock of youth.*

from the many and promote this individual to a high office in Egypt. The Biblical story of Joseph's similar promotion in Egypt is another example.

Late in the co-regency, Senenmut fell into disfavour. Perhaps he had gone too far as a commoner by building a second grand tomb close to the sacred precinct of Hatshepsut's Deir el Bahri complex, having his image sculpted into hidden parts of this temple, and using his royal connections to have Hatshepsut's artists create a red quartzite sarcophagus for his eternal life. We know that this sarcophagus was shattered into fragments. Senenmut's images at Deir el Bahri were chiselled out, his body never found. Whether Hatshepsut tired of him or he disappeared with her or survived her, we cannot yet decide.

➤ *Hatshepsut's Disappearance* ◀

After the twenty-second year of Thutmose III's reign or the fifteenth year of the Hatshepsut-Thutmose III co-regency, we have no record of Hatshepsut. Thutmose III was then on his way towards his victories in the north-east. How and why she disappeared is unknown. What can be said with any certainty is that her monuments and, in particular, her name and images were systematically destroyed by later kings. Her name was omitted from later king lists.

Hatshepsut had attempted to find a new language, imagery and understanding of the psychology, physiology and theology of Egyptian kingship and gender relations. Her beautiful and complex vision was scraped away and broken up by the hammers and chisels of vindictive rulers' servants. We can only lament this destruction and loss.

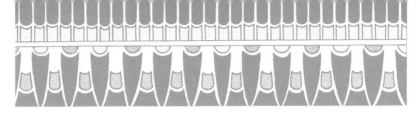

City of Akhetaten — Horizon of the Sun Disc

> ⋙ *The Pharaoh Akhenaten — an Enigma* ⋘

No ancient Egyptian has haunted our twentieth-century imagination as much as the New Kingdom pharaoh, Akhenaten (*c.*1351–1335), son of Amenhotep III. He embodies the romance of ancient Egypt for our post-modern age. A pharaoh, once mistaken for a queen,

◀ *The profile of Akhenaten's thick lips, bulbous chin, sharp nose and craning neck presents a ruler so different from the heroic warrior pharaohs before him. We are intrigued and repelled at the same time by this strange new image.*

110

Akhenaten never fitted neatly into the rigid millennial mould of his ancestors and his successors, physically, politically or spiritually. He was a ruler hated by the temple priesthoods and struck off the King Lists. Yet he was the father-in-law of Tutankhamun and the loving husband of Nefertiti, both household names now. Whatever art of his age survived his enemies' angry chisels and hammers, it still tantalises and often defies our interpretations. He simply seems so different, so out of place. Many unusual characteristics have been attributed to him — a criminal, a mystic genius, a visionary hero tragically too early for his own times, the "first individual in history", a mentor to Moses.

His unique genius has compelled writers and thinkers from different fields to seek to understand him. Sigmund Freud, beyond the strict bounds of Egyptology, identified Akhenaten as the source of Moses', and consequently the West's, monotheism. Agatha Christie wrote a play about him. Finland's Mika Waltari set a major novel, not in the dark ice forests of Lapland, but by the banks of the sunlit Nile. In our own time, Philip Glass devoted an opera to him. The Australian poet Dorothy Porter has recently crafted Akhenaten's voice into poems of lyric, edgy brilliance.

➤ *An Age of Impermanence — a King in a Hurry* ◄

Akhenaten's statues stare out at us in the silent half-light of our lack of facts about him, his family and his inner circle. So much had been systematically destroyed by later kings such as Horemheb (*c.*1322–1294 BC) and Rameses II (*c.*1279–1212 BC). Much of what had been built during Akhenaten's reign was made quickly. His was an age in a hurry. For instance, the rock tomb wall reliefs, east of his new city, had been cut out of a plaster base. Often, once the plaster had worn or been torn away, all that remained were inadequate chisel cuts where the sculptor has incised through the plaster into the rock face. He left us a barely discernible outline. This hasty construction method was forced on Akhenaten's craftsmen because they could not keep pace with the demands of the royal court. None of these rock tombs were ever finished.

▲ *Under the descending spreading rays of the Aten disc Akhenaten (left) is enjoying the company of his wife, Nefertiti and their daughters. This playful family scene with Akhenaten's distended belly and thin, almost sickly arms differs dramatically from previous art depicting royalty.*

It was an age of impermanence, of sudden changes, all too quickly reversed and eventually thoroughly destroyed. What has been left behind on the walls are the faintest outlines. It is tempting for us to cut deeper, to create our own imaginative chisel strokes to make up for our incomplete knowledge. We must be careful reconstructing Akhenaten's world, but not shun the challenge of Akhenaten and his new city, Akhetaten — his "Horizon of the Sun Disc".

▲ *The richness of the royal court of Amenhotep III is revealed by the elaborate layered wigs and golden jewellery worn by two of his lesser wives — crowns, earrings, collars and bracelets. A gazelle emerges from the centre of each of their crowned foreheads with a pair of high plumes rising above each gazelle.*

⤞ *The Climax of Egypt — Reign of Amenhotep III* ⤝

The military campaigns of Akhenaten's great-great-grandfather, Thutmose III, into Syria and Nubia had secured for Egypt unprecedented power and prestige in the eyes of foreign rulers. Wealth in the form of gold, electrum, silver, lapis lazuli, turquoise, copper, bronze, furniture, vases, cereals, fruit trees, cattle, sheep, horses, chariots, were borne into Egypt on the shoulders of thousands of slaves. The god who delivered the New Kingdom pharaohs their distant victories, Amon-Re, was rewarded.

◀ *Strength, confidence and determination line the regal features of Amenhotep III's Great Wife and mother of Akhenaten, Tiye. Amenhotep's devotion to Tiye was celebrated when he had a great lake and pleasure boat constructed for her private use, a series of scarabs to celebrate their marriage, and a pair of colossal statues, enthroned together, with the queen the same size as the king.*

His temples grew larger. His priests multiplied. The great grandson of Thutmose III, Akhenaten's father, Amenhotep III (*c.*1387–1350 BC), enjoyed these animal, vegetable, mineral, metallic and human riches carried into Egypt for three generations before him. He presided over a universal peace as the greatest king in the world — Lord of the Two Lands at the climax of Egypt's power. His forces commanded the roads and sea lanes well beyond Egypt's natural frontiers. He married princesses from Syria, Mitanni and Babylonia. But no daughter of his would marry a foreigner! He was the "Sun King" of his age, known as the "Dazzling Sun Disc", "King of Kings".

While building sacred structures for Amon-Re, he asserted the stamp of his absolute authority. His builders at Karnak dismantled earlier shrines scattered between Thutmose I's pylon and the river wharf. Their stones formed the fill of his great pylon. It was planned that this massive structure would form the great final gate of the Karnak temple. Amenhotep III had a canal and a small lake dug to round off the completion of his mighty edifice, where Nile and temple met. He saw himself as the king who completed Karnak.

The "Dazzling Sun Disc", Amenhotep III, proclaimed his power by producing many scarab beetles to distribute to the far limits of his domain.

One of these scarab publications announced his marriage, not to a "God's Wife of Amon", a princess from the royal household, but to a commoner from Middle Egypt, whose name was Tiye. She would be his "Great Wife". Together they presided over a glittering and beautiful court. In festival after festival, the king was celebrated with imperial pomp and circumstance.

✺ Sunset — the Death of Amenhotep III ✺

The luxury and ease of this festive royal court took its toll on Amenhotep III. His mummified remains reveal him to have been bald, old and overweight. His mouth was lined with severely worn teeth, his gums bloated with abscesses. He died seven months after the Mitannian king, Tushratta, the brother of one of his wives, had sent him a sacred statue of the goddess, Ishtar, to cure his ailments. She failed. The falcon, that is Amenhotep III, "flew to heaven". His son, Amenhotep IV (c.1351–1335 BC), became the living Horus. This high noon of the "Dazzling Sun Disc" had past. Egypt had entered a new age.

✺ The King and the Sun Disc ✺ — Amenhotep IV Becomes Akhenaten

We know little of Amenhotep IV's upbringing, but he could not have avoided the sun worship at his father's court. An image of the sun became the young man's fixation. This was not the sun compounded with Amon of Thebes, King of Gods, Amon-Re, it was an aspect of the sun known as the Aten, the Sun Disc. It held the king in awe beneath its perfect circle, surrounded by the splay of its long rays, fanning out over the sovereign. These sun rays end in human hands. They hold up signs of life, a series of *ankhs* (hieroglyph for life), to the raised faces of the king, his queen Nefertiti, and their daughters. In image after image, the rays and *ankhs* only extend to the royal family.

Only the king knows the Aten. Only the king can reveal the Aten to humankind. He is the god of each individual. He has become the *akh* (glorious spirit) *en* (of) the Aten — Akhenaten, "Glorious Spirit of the Sun Disc". Early in his reign he left Thebes and headed down the river in quest of the "Horizon of the Sun Disc" — *Akhet* (horizon), of the *Aten* (Sun Disc), Akhetaten.

◀ The high Aten extending its long rays down on Akhenaten and Nefertiti. Only the royal family experienced the Sun Disc's life-giving power. The Aten, the king and the queen formed a unique co-regency. The king passed on the brilliance and blessings of the Aten to the rest of humankind.

➤ One God Against the Many ◀ — Triumph of the Sun Disc

Akhenaten's new order was a reversal of what Egyptians had taken for granted. He had changed the old balance of Egyptian religious life. Egyptians had always lived in a harmonious tension between, on the one hand, a multitude of ancient gods who had their own particular places of power and worship, and on the other, a growing awareness that a singular divine force moved the universe. The many were in harmony with the one.

Akhenaten used his kingship to break the cherished Egyptian reverence for their old beliefs and practices. He simplified Egypt's spiritual framework. Like the warrior pharaoh, Thutmose III who, at Megiddo, stood alone against his cautious advisers, against the chaotic panic of foreigners and was let down by his own soldiers, Akhenaten constructed a parallel framework of Bronze Age heroism. The restless energy that Egypt had once expended on distant battlefields, that impelled them to the edges of the world, was now channelled onto another level of experience.

Egypt's religious profusion of gods and bewildering mythologies were swept aside. One divine power, manifest in the Aten disc, lit Akhenaten's mind. There would be no shadows of confusion in his Egypt.

➤ New Sacred Site — Akhetaten ◀ — Horizon of the Sun Disc

The site of Akhenaten's new city reflected a shift to a new sense of the divine. Egyptian geography was an intricate pattern of sacred sites. So much of Egypt was holy to individual gods. Amon had Thebes, Re Heliopolis, and Horus Edfu. Akhenaten, however, had found a space in Middle Egypt, empty of any sacred significance — no god, no temple, no

altar. There was only the sloping shape of the cliffs on the Nile's east bank to hint that this horizon, *Akhet*, would belong to the Aten. This was the horizon of the Aten: Akhetaten.

Here Akhenaten created an arena to display himself as a heroic king, animated by the Aten, the Sun Disc, on the one god's horizon. Here the king could radically reverse the spiritual orientation of the Two Lands.

He reigned in a co-regency with the Aten. For the first time in Egyptian history a god was named inside royal cartouches. Akhenaten placed his own royal names in smaller cartouches beside the Aten's. This unique co-regency was perhaps widened to include Akhenaten's great queen, Nefertiti. She was even pictured alone with the Aten.

The king and his courtiers were to be buried on the east bank of the Nile, in rock tombs, east of Akhetaten. The complex mythology of the *Am Duat* and the *Litany of Re* were abandoned. The Egyptian underworld was abolished. The afterlife at

◄ *After the early distorted, beguiling portraits of the king, the royal sculptors had taken to heart the new teachings of Akhenaten. They began to sculpt the wonders of the world lit by the Aten. This beautiful bust of Nefertiti with its exquisite balance of precision and sensuality is testimony of their belief and skill.*

Akhetaten was aligned with sunrise, not sunset. It was designed to be in the perpetual sunlit presence of the Aten and Akhenaten.

Akhenaten had previously built a temple at Karnak to the Aten. But he did not continue in the tradition of his dynasty by extending the existing structure to the west. Instead, he raised a new edifice to the east in the opposite direction of his ancestors. His temples to the Aten were built without roofs, with an open field of tables piled with breads, beer, meats and fruits. They were offered to the life-giving rays of the Disc. The darknesses of Amon's Karnak temple were now sundered by the radical light of his reforms.

⇒ *Freedom of Expression* ⇐ *in Art and Literature*

Egyptian art flourished under Akhenaten. At Akhetaten, German archeologists found the famous bust of Nefertiti in the house of the sculptor, Thutmose. After the early exaggerated, distorted figures on wall reliefs or as statues, Akhenaten's artists softened their approach to produce works whose exquisite individuality and beauty continue to amaze us today. They express a new, direct revelation of nature, released from the earlier, formal constraints of Egyptian art. It almost seems that

▶ *Artists were an essential part of the community at Akhetaten. It seems the artists were instructed by Akhenaten himself, as Bek the sculptor claimed. In his own stele, Bek carved himself with the pot-bellied shape characteristic of Akhenaten.*

Akhenaten's ideas liberated the genius of his artists. They saw things as they were, lit by the Aten, inspiring a more sensual, intimate rendering of figures. We are presented with touching scenes from the daily life of the royal family, Akhenaten and Nefertiti kissing. They play with their children. They grieve for a dead daughter.

The Great Hymn to the Aten, written on tomb walls east of Akhetaten, must have inspired artists. It was almost certainly written by the king himself. In it we have the language of daily Egyptian life, Late Egyptian. First used fleetingly by Hatshepsut earlier, now Akhenaten used it more freely throughout the hymn. The old classic formality of Middle Egyptian was gone.

A tender, new voice had entered Egyptian literature. Akhenaten's god was in direct contrast to Thutmose III's. Amon-Re guides his son's arm as Thutmose III smites Egypt's enemies and steals the very air from their nostrils. In the *Great Hymn to the Aten*, all peoples — Egyptians, Syrians, Nubians — are one under the love and care of the Aten which cherishes every element of nature from the mighty Nile to the tiny chick being hatched. Here is a god, all powerful and all loving, radiant over the entire world, embracing all of humankind in the unifying span of its rays.

▶ *This statue has caused much controversy. It has been argued that Akhenaten is kissing his wife Nefertiti, or one of his daughters, or even his co-regent, Smenkhkare. Recent opinion tends towards one of his daughters.*

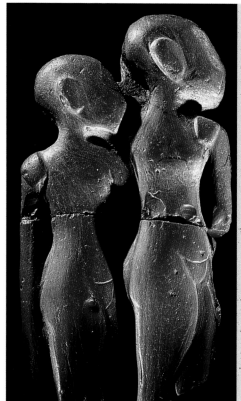

◀ *These sculpted red glass figures are believed to be princesses from Akhetaten. With one hand each they clasp the other's shoulder in a uniform gesture of raised heads, typical of Akhenaten's art. Perhaps they gaze at their parents under the dazzling Aten.*

▼ *This wall painting shows Akhenaten's daughters playing with a duck. Their amusement is animated by the free, liquid features of their long, black-rimmed eyes and their elongated red heads.*

121

◄ *One of the Aten's rays ending in a hand reaches down to the earth. Here is a detail of the dramatic moment when the Aten blesses the natural world with its life-giving light as* The Great Hymn to the Aten *proclaimed.*

➤ Royal Road of the Horizon of the Aten ◄

A long direct way, the Royal Road, connected the king's residence in the north to the Central City. It formed a straight spine over undulating terrain. True to the graphic contours of the hieroglyph *akhet* which means horizon, the Royal Road followed the land's natural undulations, sloping down away from the king's residence in the North City, soundly lodged below a cliff face close to the river.

Then the road rose toward the heights of the King's House and the temples set on the plateau of the Central City. The gently rolling road linked the ends of Akhenaten's capital. The king appeared along this road on his chariot, his loving queen beside him, as if riding the hieroglyph *akhet* — the *akh* (glorious spirit) of the Aten (Sun Disc) travels the *akhet* (the horizon) of Aten: Akhenaten at Akhetaten.

► *The close relationship between Akhenaten and the Sun Disc is evident in this regal bust. The king is covered by the Aten's double cartouche. This intimate contact with the Aten's royal names highlights the co-regency between the king and the Sun Disc.*

⇒ *Bread of Akhetaten — Gifts of Akhenaten* ⇐

A common scene on Akhenaten's officials' tomb walls sets the king above his courtiers. He stood at a balcony in a courtyard of the King's House in the Central City. There he distributed gifts in another display of royal power. Not only was gold given, but also the officials' rations, such as bread. This emphasised their dependence on the king.

They were not the only subordinates of Akhenaten. The king controlled the temple's wealth. Unlike other New Kingdom temples, there were no large granaries inside Akhetaten's sacred precincts. They were to be found in the King's House. Ovens have been excavated just outside the Aten temples. However, other New Kingdom temples did not have ovens for baking. Akhenaten used the bakeries adjoining the temples to bake bread as rations royally rewarded to his followers.

⇒ *Life in the Suburbs* ⇐

Apart from some officials who lived close to the royal North City, most of Akhetaten's population inhabited large residential areas north and south of Central City. Some officials lived far from the king. This was a society of commuters. They drove by chariot to the king or Central City.

Their housing estates shared similar ground plans centred on a square

within the house. In this living room the owners welcomed their visitors. At least one column supported the raised ceiling. Windows were fitted in the upper parts of the walls, with a place set aside for washing. Other spaces spread out from this centre — a

◀ *Mystery surrounds the identity of this serene, alabaster face. Many of the names and figures in the tomb where this bust was found, were erased. It is most probably, Kiya, another wife of Akhenaten, part of the glittering court at Akhetaten.*

▲ *The outlines of the village houses are inscribed on this block, once part of Akhenaten's temple at Karnak. The houses of Akhetaten's suburbs would have had similar front doors, flat roofs, storage vaults, windows and stairs leading up to the roof as well as goats and dogs dashing about the desert wilds beyond the village.*

▶*After Akhenaten's death during Tutankhamun's reign, for a brief, shining moment there was harmony between Aten and Amon-Re. On his golden throne Tutankhamun and his queen, Ankhesenamun, are showered by Aten's rays. Later any memory of Akhenaten and his god was cursed and destroyed.*

reception room, closer to the entrance; storage areas; and more private rooms, including the main bedroom, perhaps with a bathroom and toilet. It must be remembered, there was no public sewerage network. Disposal of waste was primitive.

A stairway usually led to the house's flat roof. This large space was used as a summer bedroom and for storage. There may also have been an upper room, perhaps used by the women of the household.

Outside the house and inside the property's walls, with an entrance for chariots, were sheds for livestock, granaries, a tree-lined garden, perhaps workshops (Nefertiti's bust was found in Thutmose the sculptor's home), a shrine and some living quarters. The kitchen was located downwind outside, so the breeze did not blow smoke back into the house. Each compound had its own well. Water was not supplied directly from the river.

At Akhetaten these building complexes were not quiet, dormitory suburbs. They were essential to an economy without money — surplus

grain, animals, workshops. They generated much waste. The Akhetaten suburbs were punctuated with rubbish piles.

There was no physical separation between social classes. The pattern of their houses was similar. They did differ in size. The distinct separation in society was between the king, who lived in the isolated North City behind large, imposing walls, and the rest of the people.

➤ *The Horizon Abandoned — a City in Ruins* ◄

The Akhetaten community was dependent on the king. His Royal Road was the central city axis. He supplied his subjects with rewards such as gold, but often with their bread. When he died the focus of his city went with him. There was a short interim period under his successor, Tutankhamun, when the residents stayed on.

Yet within a generation Akhetaten was abandoned. It was a city whose memory was cursed by later Egyptian generations, untouched for over 3000 years, waiting for our age to excavate its silent desert ground to reveal again the city of Akhetaten — Horizon of the Sun Disc.

◄ *Like this superb, unfinished bust of Nefertiti, the reign of Akhenaten remains to intrigue, tease and haunt our imaginations with what might have been had the king lived longer to consolidate his reforms.*

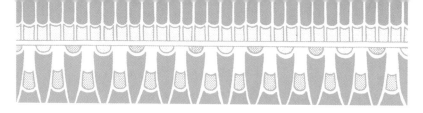

Sunrise at the Edge of Forever

⋗ Secret Transfers — the Royal Mummies ⋘

By the end of the New Kingdom (*c*.1070 BC), Egypt was collapsing into chaos. The work of the heroic earlier centuries was being undone. Egypt's armies were divided and at odds with each other. Foreigners stalked the Two Lands again. Temple complexes became refuges for ordinary people, fearful of violence on all sides. The villagers of Deir el Medina sheltered behind the walls of Rameses III's mortuary temple. The spectre of famine haunted Egypt. Its economy was severely strained and racked with inflation. The tombs of the Queens were looted. Later even the secure Valley of the Kings was violated by tomb robbers.

▶ *Even Tutankhamun's tomb, hidden for over 3000 years, was violated by tomb robbers. They had stolen a statue from the young king's little gold-plated shrine. Then the tomb was resealed, to be re-opened this century.*

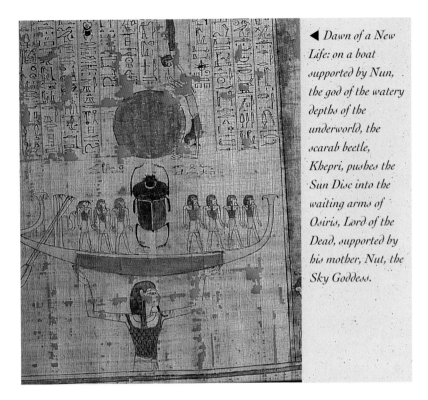

◄ *Dawn of a New Life: on a boat supported by Nun, the god of the watery depths of the underworld, the scarab beetle, Khepri, pushes the Sun Disc into the waiting arms of Osiris, Lord of the Dead, supported by his mother, Nut, the Sky Goddess.*

During this dangerous breakdown of law and order it was decided to remove the mummies of the kings, other members of the royal families and the high priests to a safer location. One of the hidden mummy nests was situated at Deir el Bahri. It was rediscovered late last century by the French Egyptologist, Gaston Maspero, containing the battered skull of Seqenenre, together with the mummified remains of Thutmose I and III, Seti I and his son, Rameses II. This was one way late New Kingdom Egyptians attempted to right the disorientation of their world. Their kings' mummies must be kept intact. Their disturbed spirits were appeased. This secret transfer was part of the ancient Egyptian hope that the bodies of their lords would endure forever, so their spirits would last for eternity in the otherworldly aura of the gods, as the transfigured sun god Re sailed through the perilous depths of the underworld toward dawn.

➤ *Mummification — the Transfiguration of the Body* ◄

It was not only the kings who had eternal life but also ordinary New Kingdom Egyptians. This era furthered a process, the "democratisation of the afterlife", which began as the Old Kingdom disintegrated. Every Egyptian lived in the hope of life after death, based on the survival of her or his physical body.

They had slowly developed a process, known as "mummification", to preserve the body after death. It began when the corpse was taken to the *ibu*, "Place of Purification", located on the Nile's West Bank, where there was access to water. Here the body was bathed with natron dissolved in water. Natron's disinfectant properties helped preserve the body. Then it was taken to the *per nefer*, "House of Perfection", where the actual mummification took place. According to Herodotus, the

5th century BC Greek historian and visitor to Egypt, the best method involved most of the brain being extracted with an iron hook. The unreachable remnants were then washed away. A flint knife cut through the deceased's side to remove the vital organs.

We now know that four of the internal organs were separately washed, dried, treated with natron and hot resin, bandaged and bundled into canopic jars. Their lids originally had human heads, but after the Eighteenth Dynasty these lids came in the form of the Sons of Horus, four gods who guarded an organ each.

◄ *Now a dark shell of preserved skin and bones — the Egyptians mummified the body to last forever as they believed their spirit or ka needed the physical body to survive forever.*

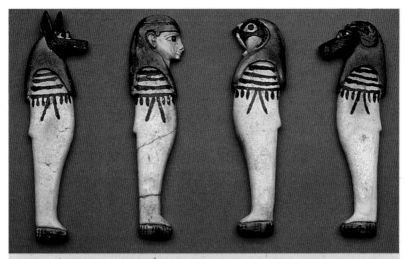

▲ *Later in the New Kingdom the lids of the canopic jars, under which the deceased's mummified organs were stored became so popular that they were also made into amulets. These lids came in the form of the Sons of Horus, four gods who guarded an organ each — Duamutef the jackal watched over the stomach; human-headed Imsety, the liver; Qebehsenuef the falcon, the intestines; and Hapy, ape-headed, protected the lungs.*

◀ *The jackal god, Anubis, was often portrayed seated upon a tomb. Jackals stalked dark, deserted cemeteries. The Egyptians saw them as guardians of the dead. Anubis embalmed Osiris — this was the first mummification.*

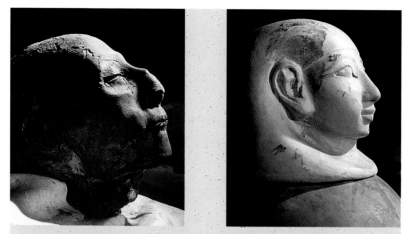

▲ *Evidence of the embalmer's skills: the mummified head of Nebra bears a striking resemblance to his canopic jar's lid, sculpted in the shape of his head while he was alive.*

This procedure was directed by the *hery seshta*, "the overseer of mysteries". He represented and perhaps wore the jackal mask of Anubis, who had, in Egyptian mythology, cared for and embalmed the deceased Osiris.

Then the body, emptied of brain and viscera, was packed on the outside and the inside with natron. Over the next forty days it lost three-quarters of its body weight. The natron was removed. After a bath in Nile water, the body shell, like the risen sun itself, was lifted out of the cleansing water, and then filled with new natron, sawdust or myrrh and resin inside linen bags to return the body to its natural shape. The incision, through which the organs were earlier removed, was stitched up. The orifices in its head were plugged.

By this stage the skin had darkened. It was rubbed with resin, which further blackened the body and sealed the skin's pores, preventing tissue deterioration. An assortment of spices was then sprinkled over the "restored" body.

Cosmetics were often then applied to fully "restore" the body's individual features. Often as many as twenty layers of bandages were

wrapped around the mummified corpse. Magic amulets and jewellery were often placed within the linen's layer. Sometimes prayers for the deceased were written onto the linen. The later layers were bound more tightly to hold the mummy's human shape. This vital part of the procedure lasted fifteen days.

Herodotus described other treatments which were less expensive. In some cases the body was not opened. Cedar oil was introduced into the body through the anus which was then sealed. After natron was externally applied for a set amount of time, the potent oil was evacuated from the corpse, along with the liquefied organs and flesh, leaving only skin and bones. The corpse was then returned to the deceased's family.

The entire mummification process, as Herodotus stated, took seventy days. This was the period the bright star, Sirius, was absent from the night sky, until it rose, just before the sun, to signal the coming of the inundation, when nature was renewed, just as the mummified body had been purified, rejuvenated, perfected and ready for burial and resurrection.

➤ The Individual's "Other" ≺ Life Forms

Why go to these elaborate lengths? Such a question would have horrified an ancient Egyptian. They understood that the physical body was not the only "body" a human being possessed. There were others, subtle and sometimes intangible, but just

◀ *To make their existence in the afterlife even more pleasant, Egyptians had model workers carved in wood, known as shabtis to work for them in the "heavenly" Field of Reeds.*

as profoundly part of the human person as flesh, blood and bones. The physical body, the *khet*, existed in a field of activity, briefly interrupted by death and intimately connected to the individual's other vital elements — *ka* (lifeforce), *ba* (spiritual manifestation), *ib* (heart), *ren* (name), *akh* (transfigured spirit) and *shwt* (shadow).

▶ *Humans were not the only living beings mummified. Especially after the New Kingdom animal cults flourished, Egyptian gods took on animal forms. Worshippers could offer a mummified animal to the god who shared its form. The cat was sacred to the goddesses Bastet and Pakhet. This mummified cat was found at Saqqara.*

▼ *On this panel of a shabti box the deceased and her ba, in the form of a bird with a human head are nourished by the life-giving waters of the goddess of the sycamore tree.*

➤ Ka — *Life Force — Parallel and Eternal* ◄

When Hatshepsut and Amenhotep III portrayed their respective Divine Births they had Khnum, the ram-headed creator god, shape two figures — their physical body and their *ka* — on a potter's wheel. The *ka* is the spiritual lifeforce standing beside the body. It animates the physical body and will survive death if the physical body is preserved and protected. Bodies are mummified to ensure the *ka*'s ordinary eternal existence. The *ka* can also inhabit statues. Long before the New Kingdom, Egyptians have placed *ka* statues in their tombs to give the *ka* a home in case anything happened to the corpse.

It is more than a spiritual entity. The *ka* enjoys life. It must be fed. When an Egyptian drank to a friend's health, he toasted the *ka*. The *ka* engendered children. A man spoke of the offspring of his *ka*. For a king it was his *ka* which mingled with the gods and empowered the sovereign of the Two Lands. Both royal and non-royal Egyptians, after death, must re-establish this crucial connection between body and *ka* that once bound them to life on earth. An elaborate art, architecture and ritual of death developed around this refusion of *ka* to body to immortality.

◄ *Villagers from Deir el Medina in the process of manufacturing a coffin (left) — one painter puts the finishing touches on the coffin's face while a kneeling worker holds the coffin still. Another coffin's face (right) is being sculpted and a man below is completing a djed column, symbol of support, stability and duration.*

⋟ *The Opening of the Mouth* ⋘ *— the Dead Return to Life*

This important ceremony was portrayed occurring outside the tomb. The body had been placed inside its coffin which was then taken to the tomb and placed upright outside the tomb door. Often it was the son of the deceased who raised an adze, among other ritual instruments, to the deceased's face sculpted on the coffin's exterior. The adze would touch the mouth, enabling the dead to speak, eat and drink, the eyes to see, the nostrils to breath, and the ears to hear. The deceased mummified body was revived. It was now a perfect vessel for the deceased *ka*.

▼ *This wall painting illustrates the ceremony of the Opening of the Mouth in front of the tomb. The adze is being lifted to the mouth of the coffin to revive the deceased mummified body. With an anubis mask, a priest holds the coffin upright before two wailing mourners.*

❧ Ba — *Winged Power — Appearance and Emergence* ❧

The *ba* could be equated to the consciousness of a person in a way, as German Egyptologist Hornung argues, that the *ka* operates on the level of the unconscious. A scribe who drinks too much beer may lose his presence of mind, his *ba*; or a panicked enemy in flight before a warrior pharaoh are deserted by their *ba*s.

The *ba* appears with a human face attached to the body of a bird. During the day the *ba* flew away from the tomb, free to roam abroad in the world, unlike the tomb-bound *ka*. It was necessary for the dead person's physical body to be rightly reunited with the *ba*. Its wings protected or embraced the dead individual. It was not a distinct parallel element of the individual, but an immortal aspect and spiritual manifestation of the person which emerges fully after death. It has physical needs, desires and potency. It enjoys food and copulation.

❧ Ib — *Heart — Seat of Intelligence* ❧

The heart was considered by the ancient Egyptians to be the seat of intelligence and reason, the fount of desire and memory, energy and decision. Here beat human emotion and free will. Naturally, it was the most important organ. It was left inside each person's mummified body.

▶ *Once the deceased has entered the realm of the afterlife he encounters his ba-soul, risen up the tomb's shaft from the depths of his burial chamber. He opens his tomb door to release his own ba, appearing with his own head and the body of a bird.*

It had to be available to the deceased when she or he came before the gods of the Judgement. An amulet, in the shape of a scarab beetle, was often inscribed with a special utterance that the heart would not betray its owner at the critical weighing of the heart on the scales against the feather of *maat*, truth. Egyptians believed that the heart could oppose, by the nature of its free will, the very order of creation and turn against the gods or its owner.

Ren — *Name — Existence and Identity*

All created things have a name, *ren*. It gave each individual an identity, an existence. Everyone was named immediately on their birth. Names have power, magic. Re, the Sun God, had a secret name. Isis tricked Re into revealing it to her. This knowledge meant that Horus, her son, would then be placed second only to Re among the hierarchy of the gods. This mythical knowledge of names is echoed in life and death. If a person's name is forgotten or destroyed, she or he can be denied immortal inheritance, rights or powers. The name *ren* opens one to identity, to existence, to eternity.

Akh — *Transfigured, Well-Equipped Spirit*

It was the aim of the dead to become an *akh*, a transfigured, well-equipped spirit, a *ba* truly bonded to its *ka*, a lustrous inhabitant of the underworld. These *akhs*, these brilliant beings were never pictured on tomb walls. They were on a distant, shining plane of experience,

◄ *In this pectoral of Tutankhamun, the protective goddess-sisters, Isis and Nephthus flank the divine beetle, Khepri, the scarab placed over the heart to ensure the resurrection of the king into a royal afterlife.*

◀ *In the hope that the wearer of this heart amulet will be reunited with his* ba, *this amulet with a human head has been carved with a* ba *bird in flight.*

detached from human imagining, dwelling beyond the horizon, *akhet*, in a place of transfiguration bathed in eternal light, a star. Here the individual could merge, as Dutch Egyptologist, Henri Frankfurt speculates, with the vast, unchanging, perpetual forces of the wheeling universe.

➤ Shwt — *Shadow* — *Power of Darkness* ◀

The deceased was empowered and protected by his *shwt*, shadow. While the *ba* bird soars in the sky, the shadow remains earthbound, appearing at the tomb door, a place of transformation, of entrance and exit. Yet both *ba* and *shwt* often appear together in the same picture, adoring Re or revivifying the mummified body, charging it with power and energy. The shadow can proceed with speed, a dark conduit of power in the underworld. Here the sun passes, casting its life-giving force on those dwelling in the nether realms. This positive, cosmic power of darkness is also reflected on the personal level. For the deceased it is latent in each immortal Egyptian.

➤ *The Tomb — a Home Forever* ◀

Ancient Egyptians built their tombs to ensure that their mummified remains would be safe and sound, to give their subtle entities — *ka, ba, ren, akh, ib* and

◀ *By the time of the New Kingdom, kings had long abandoned the pyramid as their tomb. Ordinary people now used this ancient architectural form. This picture shows the restored entrance to one of the worker's tombs at Deir el Medina.*

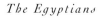

▲ *Inside the tomb of the Deir el Medina worker, Pashedu, the tomb owner reverently kneels by a date palm to drink from a pool of sacred water.*

shwt — a home forever, and to provide a place where their memory would endure among their family and friends where they could be visited and be in contact with the living.

During the Beautiful Festival of the Valley families would remain at the tomb sheltered by its walls, cooled by its gardens and starlit pool. The tomb was a place where the *ba* could retreat from the dark, uncertain night to a secure house. In the morning both the *ba* and *ka* could "come forth by day" into the light of Re. The *ba*, here, would be nourished not only by the food offered, but also by the tomb's garden shrubs and trees and its sparkling pool.

There were many types of tombs from simple pit burials in the hot, drying desert sands to the massive Old Kingdom Pyramid complexes to the long descending rock-cut tombs of the Valleys of the Kings and the Queens.

▲ *Nakht and his wife approach the Lord of the Dead, Osiris, in the pleasant surroundings of their tomb's garden and pool. The tomb was a place of tranquil beauty with trees and water to attract the tomb owner's airborne bä-soul.*

➤ The "Great Place" — the Valley of the Kings ◄

Hidden behind Deir el Bahri's towering cliff face lies a step cleft of vertical rocks, the arid, remote Valley of the Kings, known as the "Great Place". Here the Peak of the Western Theban mountain looms, like a pyramid, high on the western ridge. Far below the elaborately mummified and bejewelled bodies of the New Kingdom rulers were buried, each in a chamber known as the "House of Gold", the architectural climax of majestic halls, a deep vertical shaft and long corridors and staircases cut through the immense depths of the limestone cliff face.

These tombs, during the New Kingdom, varied from dynasty to dynasty. In the early Eighteenth Dynasty (*c*.1570–1294 BC) their winding corridors resembled the secret subterranean paths of the underworld, royal maps charting the sacred journey of the king. After the king's mummified body left the world of sunlight which is the realm of Re, it was taken down corridors named the "Paths of Re" toward the kingdom of Osiris, past the "Hall of Separation" where the terrible shaft fell away into a deep abyss. The king and Re went on to confront and defeat the monsters of the depths and secure the return of the sun to the world of the living and the dead. Then Re, Osiris and the king could be one in the climax of the tomb — the royal burial chamber, the "House of Gold". And the sun rose again. The world was saved from dark night. Each divinity — Re, Osiris and king — was restored to his own glory in the new light of day.

The Egyptians

The King Becomes a God
— the Tomb of Tutankhamun

On the north wall of Tutankhamun's burial chamber we can witness this transfiguration toward divinity as our eyes, following the figures, move from east to west, like the course of the sun. The teenage king is dressed as Osiris, facing his "son", Ay, an older man and his successor to the throne, holding the adze. Ay is performing the Opening of the Mouth ceremony on the mummified Osiris, Tutankhamun. Once all his senses are revived Tutankhamun, holding an *ankh* symbolising eternal life, is taken by the sky goddess Nut. Together with her, he travels westward along the path of Re.

His encounter with Osiris in the west is the climax of Tutankhamun's journey. He and his *ka* move toward Osiris. All three faces — Tutankhamun, Tutankhamun's *ka* and Osiris — are identical. With his *ka* holding him, Tutankhamun and Osiris embrace. They are merging into each other, in the west, becoming one — the Osiris Tutankhamun.

The process is repeated inside the king's sarcophagus. There, on his back, his feet were aligned to the east, his head to the west, close to the place on the wall painting where he united with Osiris. His face was sculpted onto the outer golden coffin. Then one exquisite golden coffin enfolded another until three coffin shells encased his mummified body and his golden death mask, and the Osiris Tutankhamun, tranquil and transfigured became the embodiment of every Egyptian's eternal hope.

▶ *Inside the three interlocking coffins of Tutankhamun the serene face of the king as Osiris — the famous Golden Death Mask — gazes into a royal eternity.*

◀ *Carved from wood this ram-headed god was one of the few objects left behind by tomb robbers in King Horemheb's tomb. The god's partly raised arms resemble a minor god of the underworld who fought the king's enemies. His clenched fists were sculpted to hold either knives or serpents to repel dark, evil forces.*

▶ *The goddess Serket wearing a scorpion on her head outstretches her arms in a gesture of protection at one side of Tutankhamun's canopic shrine's gilded walls. Inside four golden mummy-shaped figures were placed into four alabaster containers to hold lungs, intestines, stomach and liver. Each container had a top in the shape of the king's calcite bust.*

The Egyptians

⪼ The Books of the Netherworld ⪻
— the Archeology of Hell

Along the walls of the New Kingdom rock-cut royal tombs, corridors, halls or chambers, either painted or inscribed, are the majestic Books of the Netherworld such as the *Am Duat*, the *Book of Gates*, the *Book of Day and Night*, and the *Book of Earth*. They reveal the miraculous journey of the sun through the terrors and dangers of the underworld. They abound with scenes not only of sunrise and transformation but also punishment and annihilation. In Seti I's (*c*.1292–1279 BC) *Book of Gates* there are four fiery doorways. Those condemned for eternity will be cast into these furnaces to be burnt again and again. Thutmose III's *Am Duat* portrays gods spewing flames into the graves of sinners. Horus leans on a staff beside a rising snake with the infernal title: "He who burns millions".

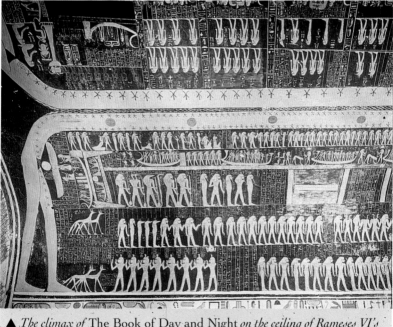

▲ *The climax of* The Book of Day and Night *on the ceiling of Rameses VI's burial chamber: the emergence of the sun between the long thighs of the sky goddess, Nut.*

In the tomb of Rameses VI (*c.*1142–1134 BC) goddesses behead bound prisoners. There are scenes on Rameses IX's (*c.*1127–1109 BC) tomb walls of the condemned painted in red and again in blue. Some are tied up, others are decapitated with knives occupying the space where their heads had once been. The blue represents nonexistence, red for blood. They kneel naked, without their genitals.

In these New Kingdom royal tombs we witness the greatness and the savagery of imperial Egypt — the charting of a course through regions as unknown and uncertain as the far reaches of the wind-swept Nile beyond the Fourth Cataract and the great waters of the Euphrates Bend, and yet it is a place of desolating pain and destruction. This is the dark psychological side of Egyptian imperialism, an early glimpse into morbid infernal regions, down into the depths of the archeology of Hell.

◀ *At the centre of this section of* The Book of the Earth *in Rameses VI's burial chamber, a fertility god surrounded by stars and sun discs stands with his erect phallus connected, along dotted lines, to each of the goddesses of the hours.*

▶ *The Sky Goddess, Nut, standing on the head of her father, Shu, god of the air, raises her arms above his towards the high Sun Disc. The Sun Disc crowns the sky and the air in this detail from Rameses VI's* Book of the Earth.

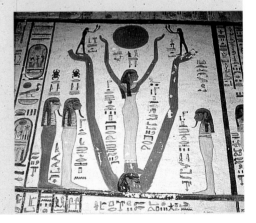

➤ The Book of the Dead ◄ — an "Ordinary" Human Journey

The ancient Egyptians never called this collection of spells or utterances to get them through the perilous trials of the afterlife, the *Book of the Dead*. For them it was the "chapters for coming forth by day". Its spells were written, drawn and printed onto sheets of papyri and tomb walls. The papyri were rolled up and placed in a small statue in the shape of Osiris or as part of the mummy's bandaging wrapped around the deceased's body.

It contains about two hundred chapters, many originating from earlier funerary works such as the Old Kingdom's royal *Pyramid Texts* or the *Coffin Texts* of the Middle Kingdom. It provided the voyager into the afterlife's "unknown country" with knowledge, certainty and hope. Various chapters deal with well-known beliefs and practices. Chapter 6 enabled the deceased to have the assistance of miniature model workers, *shabtis*, to do their afterlife duties. Chapter 30b was written on the base of heart scarabs to protect the deceased from a rebellious heart which could turn against him at the crucial moment of the Judgement: Chapter 125.

▼ *In spite of all the optimistic images of the afterlife, death in Egypt had a dreadful dimension. Here, a group of bare-breasted women mourners raise their arms in varying gestures of grief, their faces touched by sorrow, as they farewell the deceased at the beginning of the journey into the afterlife.*

➤ *The Judgement* ◄

This chapter is the most commonly illustrated section of the *Book of the Dead*. In the upper register there is a line of gods, the forty-two assessor deities. They are each from a particular place in Egypt and are each concerned with a particular sin. The deceased must name each sin's supervisory god and immediately deny committing it. The deceased is instructed to speak like this, to god after god, asserting that he had not lied, robbed, killed, been involved in homosexual acts, nor been quarrelsome, quick to anger or impatient.

Once this Negative Confession is over, the deceased is led through a hall reverberating with gods demanding recognition. He must again name these gods to pass on to the next tribunal which oversees the Egyptian instrument of justice — the scales.

Here the deceased's heart, his *ib*, is placed on one scale, the feather of Truth, *maat*, on the other. Obviously we do not possess any failures, any

▼ *The heart of Anhay is placed on the scales by Anubis against the Feather of Truth. Anhay is led toward the scales by Horus. The monster Ammit, devourer of the dead, looks on. She will eat Anhay's heart if it is found wanting on the weighing scales, and Anhay would die a "second death" with no afterlife, only oblivion.*

evidence of a heart found wanting in the balance. Otherwise the deceased would not continue toward Osiris and the Egyptian Heaven, the "Field of Reeds". Failure would have meant that his heart be tossed from the fatal scales to the composite monster goddess, Ammit, part crocodile, lion or leopard, and hippopotamus — all deadly creatures of Egypt's land and river. She would devour the deceased's heart, the sentence of a "second death", oblivion.

Thoth, the god of writing and wisdom, is on hand to record the final result. Anubis adjusts the scales, depending on whether the deceased has had an easy or a difficult life. This explains the presence sometimes of a cluster of gods around the scales themselves; related to luck (Shay), birth, nurturing and destiny (Meskhenet and Renenutet) and the birth brick itself, on to which, at a pivotal moment in his destiny, the individual was born. The scales were then judged to be in proper balance and the deceased was then announced to be "true of voice", led by Horus into the presence of Osiris who welcomed the deceased into his kingdom.

▼ *Sennedjem and his wife work in the Field of Reeds, the Egyptian "heaven". It is a well-watered world with an abundance of trees, fertile soil and bountiful crops and no snakes in the fields: this is the landscape of Egyptian hope.*

☙ *Sunrise at the Edge of Forever* ❧

In the tomb of Sennedjem, a "worker in the Place of Truth", Deir el Medina, our attention is arrested by a painting. Sennedjem stands at a vital threshold. At the top of the structure is a horizontal hieroglyph acting as a door lintel. It is a cosmic lintel, *pet*, the sky. A brilliant light pierces through the frames of the doorway. It is the radiance of the afterlife, a new dawn, a birth into immortality, symbolised by the elongated crown of wide-eyed Tutankhamun's baby head, sculpted and transfigured as the sun god, Re, emerging from the primeval mound in an open lotus, "coming forth by day". It illuminates the ancient Egyptian's entry into the otherworldly glow of the gods, the dead and eternity.

And here we stand, with Sennedjem, on the other side of Heaven's gate, waiting at the threshold of the afterlife's sunrise, at the edge of forever.

◀ *Sennedjem at the Door of Heaven: through the door posts there is a hint of a landscape — the rise of a distant mountain, part of the hieroglyph for horizon, akhet, the place where sky and earth meet. Here the sun rises and sets, life touches death. The darkness of death is lit by the light of another world. Sennedjem stands on the threshold of another life, before a mystic sunrise.*

Egyptian Chronology

The scope of Egyptian history as discussed in this book has been divided into the Archaic Period, the Old, Middle and New Kingdoms, when the ruling families or dynasties united the Two Lands of Upper and Lower Egypt. Other periods known as Intermediate Periods were times of disunity and confusion and, in the case of the Second Intermediate Period, when foreigners ruled parts of Egypt. The order of kings, mentioned in the text, are well defined, but many dates pertaining to the periods of their reign are problematic and approximate.

ARCHAIC PERIOD: DYNASTIES 0–2 (*c*.3150–2660 BC)

Dynasty "0"	(*c*.3150–3050 BC)
Horus Narmer	(*c*.3100)

THE OLD KINGDOM: DYNASTIES 3–8 (*c*.2660–2125 BC)

Dynasty 3	(*c*.2660–2586 BC)
Djoser	(*c*.2642–2622 BC)
Dynasty 4	(*c*.2586–2470 BC)
Sneferu	(*c*.2586–2561 BC)
Khufu	(*c*.2561–2538 BC)
Khafre	(*c*.2530–2504 BC)
Dynasty 5	(*c*.2475–2352 BC)
Unas	(*c*.2385–2352 BC)

THE FIRST INTERMEDIATE PERIOD (*c*.2125–2040 BC)

THE MIDDLE KINGDOM: DYNASTIES 11–12 (*c*.2040–1782 BC)

Dynasty 11	(*c*.2060–1991 BC)
Mentuhotep I	(*c*.2060–2010 BC)
Dynasty 12	(*c*.1991–1782 BC)
Senwosret I	(*c*.1971–1928 BC)
Amenemhet III	(*c*.1842–1797 BC)

THE SECOND INTERMEDIATE PERIOD (*c*.1782–1570 BC)

Dynasty 17	(*c*.1660–1570 BC)
Seqenenre II	(*c*.1575 BC)
Kamose	(*c*.1574–1570 BC)

THE NEW KINGDOM: DYNASTIES 18–20 (*c*.1570–1070 BC)

Dynasty 18	(*c*.1570–1294 BC)
Ahmose I	(*c*.1570–1547 BC)
Amenhotep I	(*c*.1552–1525 BC)
Thutmose I	(*c*.1525–1519 BC)
Thutmose II	(*c*.1519–1505 BC)
Thutmose III	(*c*.1505–1451 BC)
Hatshepsut	(*c*.1498–1483 BC)
Amenhotep II	(*c*.1454–1420 BC)
Thutmose IV	(*c*.1420–1387 BC)
Amenhotep III	(*c*.1387–1350 BC)
Amenhotep IV /Akhenaten	(*c*.1351–1335 BC)
Tutankhamun	(*c*.1335–1326 BC)
Ay	(*c*.1326–1322 BC)
Horemheb	(*c*.1322–1294 BC)
Dynasty 19	(*c*.1294–1184 BC)
Seti I	(*c*.1292–1279 BC)
Rameses II	(*c*.1279–1212 BC)
Dynasty 20	(*c*.1185–1070 BC)
Rameses III	(*c*.1183–1152 BC)
Rameses VI	(*c*.1142–1134 BC)
Rameses IX	(*c*.1127–1109 BC)

Glossary

Akh: A dead person's transfigured, glorious spirit.

Akhet: 1. Inundation season from July to October.

Akhet: 2. Where earth meets sky — horizon.

Am Duat: Book of What is in the Netherworld, painted on walls of Thutmose III's burial chamber.

Amon: One of the eight forces of chaos existing before Creation as a hidden power, later his sacred site was Thebes.

Amon-Re: A composite god who later combined the force of Re, the sun, with the power of Amon of Thebes, to become the chief god of the New Kingdom and its empire.

Ankh: Life represented by a hieroglyph with a loop rising from a T-shape.

Assyrians: A people living on the upper Tigris River who would, centuries after the New Kingdom, conquer Egypt.

Aten: The pharaoh Akhenaten's god, represented by the Sun Disc.

Atum: A form of the creator sun god, Re.

Ba: Spiritual manifestation, connected to a person's consciousness and personality, which survived death in the form of a human-headed bird.

Babylonians: A people living by the lower reaches of the Tigris and Euphrates rivers, and a later rival to Assyria.

Benben: First horizon of time and space, the "primeval mound", the place of creation.

Bes: Dwarf god of childbirth, fertility and sexual love.

Capital: The upper part of a column which widens out to support the beam above it.

Cartouche: An elongated oval of cord which magically protected and preserved the king's name, written inside it, from evil forces.

Deir el Bahri: Site of Hatshepsut's mortuary temple on the Nile's west bank.

Deshert: The Red Land, the desert surrounding Egypt.

Djer: One of the earliest rulers of Egypt, *c.*3000 BC.

Dynasty: A powerful ruling family.

Euphrates: River flowing south across Syria and Iraq to join the Tigris.

Geb: Earth god, brother-husband of Nut.

Giza: Site of the massive group of pyramids built by Khufu, Khafre and Menkaure.

Hathor: Goddess of love and fertility, consort of Horus, appearing in the form of a cow.

Herodotus: Fifth century BC Greek historian (*c*.484–420 BC) who travelled to Egypt. He wrote about Egyptian history and culture.

Hieroglyphs: Traditional form of Egyptian writing in sets of signs, known as "the god's words".

Hittites: A people from Anatolia (Turkey) who challenged New Kingdom Egypt.

Horus: Divine son of Isis and Osiris, embodied in every Egyptian pharaoh, Lord of the Living.

Hyksos: The "foreign rulers" who ruled Lower Egypt before being expelled by Ahmose, first New Kingdom pharaoh.

Ib: Human heart, seat of intelligence and free will.

Ipet-Sut: The "most-esteemed-of-places", the inner sanctum of Amon-Re's Karnak temple.

Isis: Sister-wife of Osiris, goddess of magic.

Ka: Life force.

Karnak: Site of the New Kingdom temple dedicated to Amon-Re, King of Gods.

Kemet: The Black Land: Egypt itself.

Khet: Physical body.

Maat: Goddess of Truth and Order, often represented by a feather.

maat: The concept of truth, balance and order.

Memphis: Capital of Egypt in the Old Kingdom, *c*.2660–2125 BC.

Mitanni: A powerful Near Eastern state centred on the Tigris and Euphrates, eventually defeated by New Kingdom Egypt, then by the Hittites and the Assyrians.

Mummification: Process to preserve the body after death.

Narmer: Egypt's first king *c*.3100 BC, when he united Upper and Lower Egypt.

Nekhbet: Vulture goddess of Upper Egypt.

Nile: The world's longest river running north from East Africa, eventually through Egypt out to the Mediterranean Sea.

Nubians: The black inhabitants of the regions south of Egypt's boundary.

Nut: Sky goddess, daughter of the goddess of moisture (Tefnut) and the god of the air (Shu).

Opet Festival: Most important festival on the New Kingdom Egyptian calendar.

Osiris: God of regeneration, Lord of the Dead and the Underworld.

Ostraca: Pieces of limestone flakes on which the Egyptians drew
and wrote.

Pectoral: A piece of decorative jewellery worn on the chest, counterpoised by a
pendant dropping down the back along a cord slug around the neck.

Peret: Growing season from November to February.

Pharaoh: The ruler of Upper and Lower Egypt, Lord of the Two Lands.

Pyramid Texts: Humankind's earliest surviving religious literature, *c.*2300 BC,
carved in hieroglyphs inside the chambers of the pyramids of the kings of
the late Old Kingdom.

Re: Sun god, creator of the world.

Ren: A person's name, ensuring his continued existence and identity even after
death.

Saqqara: Site of Djoser's Step Pyramid Complex.

Seth: Brother to Osiris and Isis, murderer of Osiris, and god of storms.

Shemu: Harvest season from March to June.

Shen: A hieroglyphic sign formed by a circle of doubled rope representing
eternity.

Shu: God of the air, and consort of Tefnut.

Shwt: A person's shadow.

Stele (pl. stelae) : An upright, enscribed slab, usually of stone, commonly used
by Egyptians to record their decrees, achievements and prayers.

Tefnut: The goddess of moisture who together with Shu became the first
divine couple.

Thebes: Religious centre of New Kingdom Egypt, including the Karnak
temple, sacred to Amon-Re.

Thoeris: Hippopotamus goddess, also known as Taweret, who protected
women in childbirth.

Thoth: The ibis-headed lord of time, god of writing, wisdom and magic.

Two Lands: Upper (Southern) Egypt and Lower (Northern) Egypt. They were
not united until *c.*3100 BC.

Valley of the Kings: Secluded valley on western bank of the Nile, where the
New Kingdom rulers were buried in deep rock-cut tombs.

Suggested Reading

C. Aldred, *Achenaten, King of Egypt* (London, Thames & Hudson, 1988)

C. Aldred, *The Egyptians* (London, Thames & Hudson, 1987)

C. Andrews, *Amulets of Ancient Egypt* (London, British Museum Press, 1994)

G. Callender, *The Eye of Horus* (Melbourne, Longman Chesire, 1993)

M. Demovic and M. Hayes, *Deir el Medina and Pompeii* (Melbourne, Addison Wesley Longman, 1996)

R.O. Faulkner, *The Ancient Egyptian Book of the Dead* (London, Guild Publishing, 1985)

H. Frankfurt, *Ancient Egyptian Religion* (New York, Harper & Row, 1961)

N. Grimal, *A History of Ancient Egypt* (trans. I. Shaw, Oxford, Blackwell, 1992)

G. Hart, *Dictionary of Egyptian Gods and Goddesses* (London, Routledge & Kegan Paul, 1986)

G. Hart, *Egyptian Myths* (London, British Museum Press, 1990)

S. Hellestam, "The Pyramid of Cheops as Calendar", *Discussions in Egyptology* 28 (1994) 21-27

E. Hornung, *Idea into Image* (trans. E. Bredeck, New York, Timken, 1992)

E. Hornung, *The Valley of the Kings* (trans. G. Warburton, New York, Timken, 1990)

R.M. & J.J. Janssen, *Growing Up in Ancient Egypt* (London, Rubicon, 1990)

B.J. Kemp, *Ancient Egypt, Anatomy of a Civilisation* (London, Routledge, 1991)

L.H. Lesko (ed) *Pharaoh's Workers* (Ithaca, Cornell University Press, 1994)

M. Lichtheim, *Ancient Egyptian Literature, Volumes 1* (Berkeley, University of California Press, 1973)

M. Lichtheim, *Ancient Egyptian Literature, Volume 2* (Berkeley, University of California Press, 1976)

M. Liverani, *Prestige and Interest* (Padova, Sargon, 1990)

G.T. Martin, *The Hidden Tombs of Memphis* (London, Thames & Hudson, 1991)

W.J. Murnane, *The Penguin Guide to Ancient Egypt* (London, Penguin, 1983)

G. Pinch, *Magic in Ancient Egypt* (London, British Museum Press, 1994)

S. Quirke, *Ancient Egyptian Religion* (London, British Museum Press, 1992)

S. Quirke and A.J. Spencer (eds) *The British Museum Book of Ancient Egypt* (London. British Museum Press, 1992)

D.B. Redford, *Akhenaten, The Heretic King* (Princeton, Princeton University Press, 1984)

D.B. Redford, *History and Chronology of the Eighteenth Dynasty of Egypt* (Toronto, University of Toronto Press, 1967)

N. Reeves, *The Complete Tutankhamun* (London, Thames & Hudson, 1990)

G. Robins, *Women in Ancient Egypt* (London, British Museum Press, 1993)

I. Shaw and P. Nicholson, *British Museum Dictionary of Ancient Egypt* (London, British Museum Press, 1995)

M. Stead, *Egyptian Life* (London, British Museum Publications, 1986)

E. Strouhal, *Life in Ancient Egypt* (Cambridge, Cambridge University Press, 1992)

R. Tefnin, *La Statuarie d'Hatschespout* (Brussels, Fondation Egyptologique Reine Elisabeth, 1979)

J. Tyldesley, *Daughters of Isis* (London, Penguin, 1995)

C.K. Wilkinson, *Egyptian Wall Paintings* (New York, Metropolitan Museum of Art, 1983)

R.H. Wilkinson, *Reading Egyptian Art* (London, Thames & Hudson 1992)

R.H. Wilkinson, *Symbol and Magic in Egyptian Art* (London, Thames & Hudson, 1994)

Picture Credits

Index

First published in the United States of America in 1998 by
RIZZOLI INTERNATIONAL PUBLICATIONS, INC.
300 Park Avenue South, New York, NY 10010

Reprinted 2000, 2004

First published in Australia in 1997
by Lansdowne Publishing Pty Ltd
Sydney, Australia

ISBN 0-8478-2108-0
LC 97-76004

Map illustration on page 9 by Dianne Bradley

Publisher: Deborah Nixon
Production Manager: Sally Stokes
Series Editor: Cynthia Blanche
Designer: Robyn Latimer
Project Co-ordinator: Jennifer Coren
Picture Researcher: Jane Lewis
Set in Garamond on QuarkXpress

Printed in Hong Kong by South China Printing Company